Uniforms and Boats

To

Keith

Best wishes

Davy

To
Keith
Best wishes
Davy

Uniforms and Boats

Davy Thompson

authorHOUSE®

AuthorHouse™
1663 Liberty Drive
Bloomington, IN 47403
www.authorhouse.com
Phone: 1-800-839-8640

Published by AuthorHouse   05/15/2012

ISBN: 978-1-4685-7843-0 (sc)
ISBN: 978-1-4685-7844-7 (e)

CONTENTS

In memory of my beloved Dad

&

For Fee, Lewis, Cameron & Shelley

INTRODUCTION

This book isn't a story of death and destruction, there are enough of them around by much more competent authors than I. The reason I compiled these stories will become apparent later, but they were originally for my children so I didn't want them to know what, if any bad things, Dad had done or been involved in. So no killing or bullets and bombs or even extreme violence, just a collection of memoires and stories acquired during a lifetime of wearing uniform of one form or another. Some names have been omitted to protect the guilty and for security reasons national, personal and social! Whilst most of the stories are personal, some stories regarding others have been included as they were just too funny to omit and some even legendary. As with all legends, I am confident that in some cases artistic license has been applied. Throughout the ages humanity has applied 'black humour' to deal with traumatic situations, every member of the Emergency Services and our servicemen and women will have experienced this method of 'defusing'. Outside their own working environment it would probably be frowned upon, but it serves a purposed to relieve the pressure upon those souls who day to day protect us, make us safe and unselfishly help us in our hour of need. There is a time and place for political correctness, the heat of battle or during an emergency is not the time or place. However one thing is for sure in such situations there is no racism or sexism, everyone is equal. One thing does exist in large volumes though . . . . sarcasm!

CHAPTER 1

In the beginning

On Good Friday, 14th April 1960 at the Royal Victoria Hospital, Belfast I embarked upon my life, how was I to know that I would end up married twice, have 4 children, end up wearing the uniform of all three branches of the armed forces, uniforms of other organisations and get to travel the world! I never realised what an impact the forces would have on me as an individual, or the contribution they made to a thoroughly blessed life. My affinity with, and passion for, the British Armed forces, their allies and the UKs Emergency Services will be life-long.

My ancestors and I have over 300 years of continuous service to the crown in various forms, that tradition continues today in the form of 30147137 Sapper Dean Murray, Royal Engineers, my nephew. I was raised in army married quarters and was surrounded by numerous 'aunts' and 'uncles', who actually were not related to me but we moved as a unit so they were a constant part of my life. It was obvious, a life in uniform appeared inevitable. My only sibling, a sister, is a Prison Officer as is her husband and my Father served in the armed forces, throughout the world and finished his life in uniform working for the then Royal Ulster Constabulary. One of my Fathers postings was to

Berlin as part of the NATO forces stationed in that city to deter the hordes of Communists who were living in East Germany! Let me put this in context the British Army had stationed one squadron of Chieftain tanks, 14 in total, to face the 30 or so Soviet and East German Divisions on the other side of an 8 foot wall! In fact their base, Smuts Barracks, was adjoined to Spandau Prison, infamous for housing one of the last Nazi leaders to be convicted following the Nuremburg trials at the end of the Second World War. The only prisoner was Adolf Hitler's deputy, Rudolf Hess who was guarded in turn by British, American, French and Russian troops. The Russian guard force probably had more troops than our gallant British tank force!! But we had 14 nice shiny tanks, we could have delayed the communist hordes by about, oh I don't know, ten minutes.

However the enemy were unaware that the British Army had a top secret and little known weapon in their arsenal, my Dad! Sadly I never took the time to tell him just how much of an influence he had on my personality and life in general as he passed away on 4th December 2010, but I did get the chance to tell him I loved him just before he 'marched on' and for that I'm thankful. But what a character. Born in Belfast on 14th September 1938 he lived in the docks area and as he always reminded my sister and I, in times of trouble, that he had lived through the blitz! He joined the British Army in 1961, the year after I was born, and was obviously recognised as a supreme warrior and was duly sent to 'fight' in Aden. Like all servicemen and women before him and undoubtedly those that followed there were some memories he did not wish to speak about with those that 'didn't understand' i.e. those who were not there. One of the most memorable stories my Father constantly told (and this has clearly been elaborated on at various military reunions) was of an event which took place during that tour of Aden. Given today's politically correct society undoubtedly some may find this story offensive, at the time it was practical!

My father and 2 colleagues were told to 'stag on' (go on duty) in a covert observation post (OP) to observe a main road. Part of the task was to log the frequency and type of traffic transit the thoroughfare. For anyone who has undertaken this task it is mind numbing, normally with hours of boredom interfaced with minutes of excitement when something happens! The OP was strategically placed to overlook a crossroads with a roundabout, in the middle of the bloody desert. The OP team quickly noted over a number of days that in the early hours of the morning carts with farm produce would pass the location often with the driver asleep. Reporting this back to the regimental HQ they were duly informed that this was not unusual as the carts were on their way to the local market and as the donkeys & camels had undertaken the journey regularly the drivers would load up slap the donkey or camel on the arse and fall asleep, the road was straight and the animals knew the route. Bloody clever and no need for a tacograph! As ever with periods of boredom, mischief crept in and a cunning plan was developed, their call sign was Team Alpha, you've got it, the A team! The time came to implement the cunning plan and one of the OP team stealthily made their way to the roadside near the roundabout, then as the carts, their animals and sleeping drivers approached they were silently led around the roundabout and sent home! I can only imagine the look of confusion on the face of the drivers and villagers when the carts full of local produce returned home. This 'tactic' continued for the three remaining nights that the 'A team' manned the OP. I often wondered if the animals survived! One thing is for sure the British Army really did have another cold war secret weapon in the form of my father, thinking on his feet, cunning and fearless particularly when faced with donkeys, camels, carts and sleeping Arabs.

The whole family were proud of their hero and his daring antics in defence of the realm. In 1969 his home town and country, Northern Ireland, descended into one of the longest periods of civil wars in history, although the Government were then and are today still adamant that it wasn't a war, but civil disorder, the cost of which was nearly 4000 lives. When British Soldiers started patrolling the streets of Belfast and further afield they were initially welcomed with open arms by the whole community, however that view changed and one section of the community withdrew their support. My Grandmother, still extremely proud of her daring son-in-law and like most Protestants, continued to support the Army. She was the original Mrs Doubtfire not only in attitude but in looks, I wonder if Robin Williams ever met her, probably not.

My Granny owned a large house on a street named Duncairn Gardens in North Belfast, the road was the interface between the Protestant Tigers Bay area and the Catholic New Lodge and as to be expected was a regular patrol route for the Army. Remembering that these boys were somebody's son, father or brother my Granny, who was full of kindness, decided that she would supplement the food and rations supplied by the Quartermaster! She decided she would make sandwiches and cakes etc. and flasks of tea, coffee and homemade soup and give them to the troops. However given that she lived on the 'wrong side' of the interface she would have to ensure that this support was covert. This was important as my Grandfather had unequivocally banned her from giving this support for fear of being 'burnt out', a house clearing tactic of the day! So she devised a plan whereby she would leave the 'emergency rations' at the base of her small front garden, under the cover of darkness soldiers would pick up the vital survival pack and on the return journey stash away the empty flasks and plate in their original hiding place. She was of the old school, Tupperware hadn't been invented and you couldn't just give guests sandwiches wrapped in foil, they had to be on a plate otherwise what would the neighbours think? During one of the regular house searches in the area she conveyed her initiative to a young army officer, as to be expected he was somewhat suspicious, but in true British Officer style he humoured the natives and thanked my Granny. Initially the survival packs where small but as the confidence of the soldiers grew that this was not an attempt to poison them, they became increasingly larger. This welcome respite from mess hall food continued for months without cause for concern that is until the unit patrolling the Duncairn Gardens changed! An eagle eyed soldier from the new unit spotted the suspect device at the bottom of my Grannies garden and called it in! The area was secured and the bomb disposal unit or 'Felix' (their code name) called, all this was done whilst a hysterical pensioner was mumbling something about plates, flasks and cakes. The bomb disposal unit arrived and the Explosive Technical Officer, the expert, dressed in protective clothing and resembling a Teenage Mutant Ninja Turtle, waddled towards the 'device'. The outcome of his professional assessment was that it had been deliberately well hidden, it was of a like he had never seen before and should therefore be considered a viable threat. The ensuing 'controlled explosion' broke every window in my Grannies house and several others on the street. In an effort to throw my Grandfather off the scent she had used an antique Royal Doulton plate from a collection of four, until the day he died my Grandfather believed someone from the removals company stole it when they moved to a pensioners bungalow, incidentally because republicans had tried kill British soldiers by planting a bomb at the bottom of his garden!

My Grandparents were like many, funny and confused to the end. I remember my Grandmother reporting to the local police that there where 'snoo gliffers' hanging about the local garages, the police soon worked out that it was youths sniffing glue. She once brought my Grandfather blue nylon pyjamas (nylon was all the rage at the time) he was sweating profusely overnight and the dye in the pyjamas ran, when he did not get up at his usual time she went into the bedroom to wake him, saw he was starting to 'turn blue' and proceeded to ring my uncle and announce 'George, I think your fathers dead'. So it is obvious, daftness and a sense of humour ran in the family.

During his retirement my father and three friends decided they would take a 'road trip' to Donegal, I can only imagine what was unleashed on the poor souls who resided in that part of Ireland when four old codgers descended upon them. My father and his friends drove into a petrol station to refuel only to realise they had pulled up to the pumps with the petrol cap on the side of the car furthest away from the pumps. They had decanted from the vehicle and the three passengers had entered the shop to purchase cigarettes, newspapers etc. They held the queue up until they finally realised the driver was never going to get the fuel lead to stretch to the filler cap, they duly replaced their intended purchases and went outside to help, between the four of them they still couldn't get the nozzle to reach. After ten minutes or so they decided it would be better to drive the car around to another pump. The passengers once more made their way to the shop to buy the cigarettes, newspapers etc. whilst the driver moved the vehicle. However the driver had effectively done a U turn around the pumps, he again had positioned the car with the fuelling point furthest away from the pumps, somewhat despaired his passengers, apologised, sheepishly replaced the cigarettes, newspapers etc. on the shop counter and went to the forecourt help. Having caused havoc by driving in the opposite direction to the flow of traffic, embarrassed themselves in front of a sniggering group of drivers and shop staff, the guile and quick thinking of my father's youth returned. Two passengers got into the back seat of the car and wound down the rear windows, my father passed the nozzle through the windows and out the other side to the driver who finally started to fuel, my dad rushed to the shop to pay and they left . . . . without the cigarettes and newspapers!

CHAPTER 2

Boarding School

Back to the beginning, it was due to the fact that there was no secondary school education provided for the children of service men and women posted to Berlin that I was carted off to boarding school in February 1972. A shortlist of schools where selected the most famous of which was Liverpool Bluecoats, however my Mother and Father selected a boarding school in Tywyn, Mid Wales because it was a mixed boarding and day school, it appeared homely and most importantly from my mother's perspective, the toilets were clean! I still vividly remember arriving at Machynlleth train station around 10:30 pm to be told by a very abrupt railway worker that there were no more trains until the next day, so Dad and I eventually got a taxi to Tywyn arriving around 11:00 pm. We were met by the one of the scariest woman I had ever seen, she was known as 'Matron' (I'll describe her later), she took me to a dormitory with 8 beds and Dad went to the Corbett Arms hotel for a few pints and a kip! Day one was totally confusing for me I didn't know the routine and was informed that as I kept being late I would serve detention that evening . . . . 'welcome to you new fucking home' I thought. Dad came to see me at lunch time and left for home, I began crying for a week or so! I must, at this point, describe the town on Tywyn in 1972. The place had no amenities for local children or adults other than those that had been established to part the holiday's makers from the numerous caravan sites of their hard earned cash. I still recall the aura of anticipation when the rumour got out that a swimming pool would be built in the town, you would have thought that Tywyn had been awarded the Olympic Games. The sheer delight when a family called Westlake opened a proper fish and chip shop now appears ludicrous. When the new cinema opened it was like the messiah had decided to start phase two of helping the world from Tywyn. The place was desolate. I hated every minute of boarding school, as my parents lived in Germany I spent most half term holidays in a building with no more than two other boys, the boarding school regime wasn't relaxed during these 'holidays' and the joys of Tywyn were all that we had to relieve the boredom. However there are some laughable and good memories which will stay with me forever.

On one occasion another boy and I found £80 in the main street in one of those small plastic bags that banks use for change. Like good citizens we decided to take it to the local police station the Constable at the desk was very pleasant and full of praise for two 13 year old lads who had the honesty to hand in such an amount and informed us that if the money had not been claimed at the end of six months the £60 we had handed in would be given to us. However, upon him stating that we might get the money we decided to tell another little white lie as to where we actually found the money, we stated that it had been found on the promenade some distance away from the main street. Imagine our disappointment when we returned after six months to collect our ill gotten gains to find that the money had been returned to its rightful owner who claimed it after two weeks. How the hell did that happen? We had used £20 of the original £80 we found and reported it to have been found in a totally different place, nepotism probably, Tywyn was a small community. It taught us that crime didn't pay. Another enduring memory was when a Number of Ugandan refugees came to the school, their lovable Leader the megalomaniac Idi Amin had decided the expel everyone holding a British passport and they came to the UK and were dispersed throughout the land. It was interesting doing woodwork as we would want to make the usual coffee table etc. and the Ugandan children wanted to carve things! I often wonder how those boys and girls finally integrated into the UK and if they stayed?

The obligatory boarding school ritual of 'midnight feasts' consisting of fizzy drinks, sweets and crisps were another vice which remain memorable. One day in the common room a couple of lads were playing table tennis a ball went under an upright piano in tier efforts to retrieve the ball the piano tipped, I was kneeling on a chair looking out of a window when the piano came crashing down on my right ankle, crushing it. This resulted in regular trips, over a number of months, to the nearest general hospital which was in Aberystwyth and I had to travel alone in a car with the Hag, more frightening than the doctor himself. I would get loads of letters and a phone call on Sunday evenings, after church, all of which would initially upset me and make me cry. My parents never considered that I would have to take Welsh Language or Welsh studies as a compulsory subject, what bloody help would that be? Strangely, it would be in later life wearing another uniform. The pocket money was 25p per week and normally squandered on sweets and crisps etc. this meagre amount was supplemented by doing odd jobs at weekends mainly for a local Baptist minister and his buxom wife who would pay a pittance and effectively exploit children, Christians my arse, but it was worth it for the periodic tantalising glimpse of her cleavage. To a young boy it was as good as hard core porn. The boredom was also relieved by volunteering on the Tallyllyn Narrow gauge railway, the station of which was yards from the school. We would assist in cleaning the trains and in the shop and they gave us a leather cap (a form of uniform!!!!) and free crisps and coke . . . . exploited again!

Bath night was a Wednesday and it was such events that developed my utter disgust for egg and lemon flavour shampoo and Vosene. The bathroom had four baths in it and Matron would sit in the room to ensure we all washed our hair and rinsed it properly, nothing untoward happened but it was a bloody strange ritual to a young boy. At meal times you were not allowed to leave the table unless you had eaten everything, whether you liked it or not. This included 'cooks' favourite dessert, fried jam sandwiches. No matter what you were doing or where you were going packed lunches ALWAYS contained crunchy peanut butter sandwiches. We could watch television to 6 pm then 'prep' (homework) until 8 pm after which anyone below year 5, the senior year, went to bed. Because of bloody living in Germany and boarding school I never saw Match of the Day until I was 16.

A number of 'boarders' were from military families and that meant every time a soldier was killed or injured in Northern Ireland I became the focus of their attention. I quickly learnt a number of lessons the first being to duck and weave, the second was that the funny kid didn't always get hit and the third was to look after myself. One boarder was the son of a famous explorer who accompanied Major John Blasford-Snell on his expeditions all over the world in particular to the Amazon Jungle and Africa, some others were from Civil Service Overseas families and the remainder were from families who had busy lifestyles and could afford to send the kids off. We were looked after by 'Matron' an ageing deeply religious lady, about five foot tall who wore a ginger wig and had varicose veins that should have been recorded in the Guinness Book of World Records. Frighteningly she regularly displayed an apparent hatred of children, especially boys, we called her the 'Hag' and to us children she was every bit as demonic as the word suggested. She scared me shitless and I still get the shivers to this day at the thought of her. Her one aim in life appear to be to get us to 'Chapel' every Sunday morning and evening, something we would try to avoid at all costs. For most 11-15 year olds church is boring and even more so when you're forced to go. We prayed for everything, for getting served meals, for God not ending the world whilst we ate our meals, for the hot water for our baths, everything! I still pray to this day but using the voice in my head and normally once a day. She was obsessed with church and was more like a bloody Christian fundamentalist, any task that we had to complete we were coerced into thanking God for. The Church in Tywyn was subject to a scandal covered in the National newspapers a number of years later, I can't recall the exact details but it wasn't nice. The Vicar should have prayed that he didn't get caught!

The number of 'boarders' diminished over the years and somehow, in 1975, I ended up as the 'Head Boy' of the boarders. I didn't realise I would have such an impact, the boarding school element closed that very same year, but after I had left! Prior to leaving school we had the usual round of careers conventions and whilst traditionally many from the school went into farming or engineering with Rolls Royce. I was wholly focussed on the armed forces and would travel to Wrexham to the various recruitment offices to explore careers. It was because my Father appeared to be the perfect soldier I had convinced myself that I shouldn't join the army because I wasn't sure I could be as good a soldier as he would have wanted me to be and I didn't want to let him down. I probably would have ended up trying to get into the same regiment as him as well, so everyone I knew would know how shit at soldiering I was if I failed. I regretfully found out many years later that in choosing the Royal Air Force over the Army as a career I would let him down anyway. But he kindly hid his own disappointment and supported my decision. I would not be able to 'sign on' until September 1977 due to my age and chosen RAF trade . . . . Motor Boat Crewman or to the uneducated a deckhand on an Air Sea Rescue Launch. A uniform and a boat.

In the interim period my Dad was able to get me a job working for the Army in Berlin. The chosen RAF career and the interim employment were as a result of me being quite a competent swimmer, I was the county champion at both breast stroke and butterfly and even went to the nationals in Port Talbot, South Wales where I won, but because I wasn't a native Welshman I couldn't go any further in the competition. The job my Father had secured for me was working for the Royal Engineers as a crewman on a safety boat, called 'Dobbin', during military exercises on the River Harvel. Yes my first boat! These Royal Engineer exercises involved 'heavy ferries' a mode of transporting heavy equipment over rivers, the exercises were not only designed to practise skills but also to scare the on looking communist hordes who vigilantly watched over us, from their watchtowers. I often wondered how many of those elite conscripts saw the exercises, thought "to hell with this" and decided to go AWOL home to Moscow, not many. I loved this first taste of working life, however it was short lived as the Queen had decided that the cunning and daring of my Dad was required in the German town of Osnabruck, so they posted him and as a 'minor' I couldn't stay in Berlin unaccompanied, so I moved with my family. On a positive note it got us further away from the communist hordes and should they decide to attack as it was only 150 miles run to the English Channel and then the Promised Land was only a 22 mile swim! Oh and our new neighbour in Osnabruck was about 21 and had huge tits.

As always my Dad wasn't one to have me hanging about and through his contacts got me a job with NAAFI as a store man so I could earn some money whilst learning to iron, bull boots and waiting to join the RAF. The staff at the store were great and I enjoyed my short time with them, especially the regular staff parties. I lost my virginity at one of them! I would get extra money to baby sit for my little sister who was now 8 years old and could tell the time. This is an important fact because to get her to go to bed early I'd suggest we play hide and seek, she would hide and I wander around shouting 'where are you' whilst putting all the clocks in our flat forward to within 15 minutes of her agreed bedtime. I'd find her, congratulated her for hiding so well, give her a drink, she'd go to bed and my girlfriend, Sally, would arrive. I was supposed to be saving up for my imminent departure to the RAF, but found out that girlfriends are expensive, especially when you're trying to get their knickers off. Having lost my virginity joining the RAF was, for a few moments, the last of my priorities only because I'd have to go through all that bloody expense and numerous awkward moments of misreading signals before it happened again. I have never been able to fully understand the signals that females transmit.

The time soon arrived when I had to leave NAAFI and Sally to join the RAF. Dad told me it would be an adventure and I'd find myself. This was a complete surprise to me as up until then I hadn't even known I was bloody lost. His advice to me as I departed was simple, breathe! He knew nothing about 'Crab fats'. 'Crab fat' is a term of mocking endearment used by the Army and the Royal Navy for their colleagues in the RAF. It was originally coined by Royal Navy personnel. It is alleged the reason the RAF are called crab fats by the Royal Navy goes back a many years and lies in the fact that naval personnel, in the form of Royal Marines, used to use the grease that the gun shells were caked in to get rid of crabs which they had picked up after visiting some brothel overseas. The term crab fat derived from the grease they used, it happened to be the same colour as the RAF uniform.

CHAPTER 3

Swinderby and Beyond

Its 09:00 on Tuesday September 20th, 1977, wet and strangely cold and I find myself in the Royal Air Force recruiting office in Lincoln. It is the 263rd day and 38th week of the year and Elvis Presley was at number one in the charts (remember them?) with a song called 'Way Down'. I am accompanied by nine other spotty youths who appear petrified and are being towered over by a Flight Sergeant of gargantuan proportions. I remember thinking if the RAF posted him to RAF Gatow (Berlin) he would frighten the communist hordes, he was apparently on my side and he frightened me. In all honesty I just wanted him to be somewhere else; I was too scared to move. Upon arriving at the recruiting office his opening words, which were scowled, 'Sit down and shut up', I hadn't said a word! We were told how we would be contributing to holding back the communist hordes and how we were the elite band as not everyone got into the RAF, what a proud history the service had and that the following six weeks would either be the making of us or destroy us. In the Flight Sergeants view that would mean most of us being destroyed, shattered by these revelations one potential recruit asked to go to the lavatory and was promptly told no. He subsequently pissed himself, started crying, was marched to the front door of the recruiting office and promptly told to 'fuck off'.

I thought I better stay quiet and quickly improve my water retention, I couldn't fuck off I was in Lincoln my family lived in Germany and my Dad only gave me £20 and the 200 Embassy number I, I was allowed to get on a British Army of the Rhine (BAOR) ration card.

Upon the arrival of a further 3 recruits we were marched into a separate room which was emblazoned with RAF flags, pictures of Lancaster Bombers, Spitfire, Harriers, Helicopters and the Queen. A Plaque on the wall displayed the solemn oath of allegiance we were about to take to officially make us members of the RAF. In true RAF tradition I had developed an early escape plan, I thought that I could get away from the monster Flight Sergeant if I pretended the oath on the wall was an eye test chart and I said that I couldn't read anything after the third line, the RAF would think I was half blind, stupid and send me home. Then again I was 17 and the thought of being shot by firing squad for treason was even more frightening so I gave in and read the oath. Wow, talk about comradeship, the Flight Sergeants attitude changed immediately the *attestation* took place. I became J8136665 Aircraftsman Thompson. He informed us we were no longer civvies, we were now erks and our arses belonged to the Queen. I have had the privilege of meeting our Monarch on a number of occasions but have never had the audacity to ask her why she collected backsides. As I was now a comrade in arms I felt confident to ask if I could use the toilet, I was told I could as long as I didn't climb out the window and go AWOL,

That's the thing about the armed forces you do get permission to do things but there's always a caveat.

We then boarded a green bus and embarked towards RAF Swinderby, the Royal Air Force Recruit Training Centre. It loomed out of the September mist and appeared vast; little did I know that I would become familiar with every part of the perimeter fence after having to run around on numerous occasions, mostly for minor indiscretions but on the odd occasion as part of a cross country run. Having lived in Berlin and being roughly aware of how many tanks the communist hordes had, I was not sure whether or not we were being made fit to fight or practising to run as away as far as possible in the ten minutes our gallant troops and their 14 tanks bought us.

After passing through the gates of RAF Swinderby and disembarking the bus we were shepherded into a large aircraft hanger along with around 40-50 other recruits and allocated 'Flights', I was to be in number 9 flight. Once our names had been checked and our flights allocated were we marched, and I use that term very loosely, to our 'blocks', the RAF term for accommodation. As we passed other flights who were further into their training they would whistle the theme tune to Laurel and Hardy or to the then uneducated the Dance of the Cuckoos. Our Flight Sergeant was not as big as the one in the recruiting office, but he was just as scary. We were allocated a 'bed space' and told to be outside in 10 minutes. Again we were marched, no herded, towards the camp barber and all given haircuts to make us more service like. We were then taken to the Dining Hall and fed; it soon became very clear why my Granny decided to supplement the rations of the British Army. Food in the forces is ok, but due to 'portion control' there wasn't a lot of it, you would have thought I had asked the cook if I could take his Mum out to the camp disco with the look he gave me when I asked for another roast potato. I quickly recalled some additional advice my Dad had given me before I left home, 'never fall out with the cooks or store men they can seriously fuck up your day'. We then went off to get our medicals. Day one over what a joy.

Day two started with the Tannoy system belting out Reveille at the ungodly hour of 06:30, I thought the communist hordes had come early and I was neither dressed nor trained to repel them. Thank God the Flight Sergeant came in and resolved he situation by yelling we had 5 minutes to get outside. We were once more herded off to stores to get our initial uniform issue. I was measured, poked and prodded but by breakfast I had a whole new wardrobe which was clearly fashionable as everyone was wearing the same! As I stated earlier part of my dad's preparation for me leaving was to learn how to 'bull' boots and how to iron a uniform, 'it will give you a head start' he said. Wrong Dad, it made me a smart arse in the eyes of my new found comrades, time to duck and weave! The days became repetitive. The first two weeks were basically spent learning how to move as a 'body of men', in other words we were taught to march. This was interjected with regular bouts of physical training which would prepare us for repelling the communist hordes. At this stage in the cold war we would have had to have a 'march off' as nobody had deemed us ready to handle a firearm. But the day eventually came we were to be shown the standard issue Self Loading Rifle, or SLR for short. This was 9 lbs 9 ozs of killing stick which we had to regularly hold in our arms above our heads and slowly raise and lower by our wrists shouting "9 lbs 9 ozs", a tactic known as "pokey drill". We were apparently increasing our 'muscle memory' by undertaking this task. I was concerned as I had watched the Olympic Games and the communist hordes had much bigger muscles than us, and that was just the women! At one point we were told were going to be 'gassed', Christ I thought, we must be bad. However this was standard military training and was to prepare us should the communist hordes use gas on us. We were herded into a small brick building on the perimeter of the base wearing our Nuclear, Biological and Chemical warfare suits or 'Noddy Suits' as they became to be known and respirators (the official military term for a Gas Mask). Once in this building our instructor ignited a CS gas pellet and were then instructed to moved round in a circle after a period of time we were further instructed to remove the filter canister and then screw it back on, this was to teach us how to replace the canister in times of need. As to be expected some of the less dexterous of the recruits struggled with this and the odd cough began to emerge. As the frequency of the coughing increased our instructor took us, one by one to the door and told us to remove the respirator and quote our name rank and number, we had only been in three weeks and some of us couldn't remember our service numbers, the instructor waited until such poor unfortunates appeared to be at deaths door and then let them out. This gave the rest of us an opportunity to recall and practise reciting our RAF service number prior to getting to the exit. We thought we were being clever, however upon articulating my name rank and number perfectly, he asked me to repeat it, he then asked me where I was from. Now this interest in ensuring my details were correct and my ancestry was acceptable were a nice touch but he could have waited until I was outside the gas chamber, I got outside and emptied the contents of my stomach all over my nice new Noddy suit. It is no longer acceptable in the forces but in those days there was a technique called 'beasting' this entailed giving a recruit or a group of recruits physical training until they either spewed up or passed out, for many this happened simultaneously. The forces are now more diverse with recruits but it was a different case in the seventies. I remember one recruit having the surname Gay, the Flight Sergeant drew on his spectacles with a china graph wax pen and named him 'Tit', unlucky for the poor bastard that name stuck. In the hanger on day one a member of our reception team shouted to the assembled crowd that he "didn't like black bastards", this was allegedly a reference to people that did not wash and shower, there were none white recruits in that hanger and today the same member of staff would be sacked. It really was a different time, after one of the camp discos one of the older lads had been lucky enough to get his leg over a member of the Women's Royal Air Force (a WRAF), he wasn't caught but the word got out and on the parade square a couple of days later it was announced to all and sundry that "Man who fuck WRAF, too lazy to wank" it just wouldn't be tolerated now and rightly so. Female members of the armed forces are now armed and in theatre with their male colleagues they deserve more respect than that.

There were no trainee WRAFs at Swinderby there were only trained WRAFs at the camp and they used different facilities to us 'recruits'. You couldn't even get a beer if you were under 18, the RAF had issued those who were eligible to buy alcohol with green shoulder tabards, yes if you were 18 and over you could buy a drink . . . . for yourself . . . . the caveat was that it was expulsion if you were found buying it for anyone else. After 4 weeks we were allowed out into Nottingham and got beer there, and we consumed Polo mints by the bucket load on the return journey so as not to get caught smelling of alcohol. Well that's what we thought, upon returning to camp via a pub called the Halfway House, the duty guard at the gate checked our ID cards seen we were slightly wobbly and promptly with sarcasm advised us that 'Crème de Menthe was a drink for fannies'!

One of my most enduring memories of RAF recruit training was the number of inoculations I received, the RAF clearly had plans to send me to every trouble spot in the world, imagine my disappointment when I ended up primarily serving at Plymouth and Tenby, South Wales! And so it continued for 6 weeks learning General Service Knowledge, how to salute, marching, physical training, weapons training, coping with sleep deprivation, supplementing rations via the NAAFI until we reached the final and sixth week. Being a service child I had always thought NAAFI stood for Navy, Army, Air Force Families Institute, it was only when I joined the RAF that I realised that servicemen and women knew the real meaning—No Ambition And Fucking Interest. I had nearly finished recruit training and hadn't been destroyed as the recruiting Flight Sergeant had thought, not only that I had been able to hit a 4 foot high target from 100 yards with a 7.62mm Self Loading Rifle with a good grouping and had therefore been awarded my 'marksman' badge. Bring on the communist hordes; if they stood still for a while at a distance of no more than 100 yards we might well win!!! The focus of all our attention was now on the glamour of our passing out Parade, back to the ironing and bulling. I was lucky, 9 Flight had been awarded the Champion Flight trophy and various other minor inter flight trophies, but as the Champion flight we were chosen to give the General Salute to the dignitaries during the passing out parade. The other flights got to clean the camp whilst we had extra drill. As my Dad was also a regimental drill instructor I knew he would be proud of me. He did remind me after the parade that although we had done ok, "Crab fats can't march".

CHAPTER 4

RAF Uxbridge and beyond

As the Champion Flight we were also chosen to represent the RAF at the annual Festival of Remembrance at the Royal Albert Hall, so instead of us going straight to our respective Trade Training camps, to learn our specialised skill set, we were despatched to RAF Uxbridge in London to prepare for the event. We [9 Flight], were veterans of six weeks service and the RAF had chosen us because of our marching skills to represent them at a very important national memorial service watched by millions of TV viewers, WRONG. RAF Uxbridge is the home of the Queens Colour Squadron (QCS) of the RAF Regiment, they are arguably the best of all three services when it comes to drill and put on what is probably the best 'silent' drill demonstration in the world, but they also complete Ceremonial duties at Buckingham Palace. But that's not their day job they are also highly trained infantry soldiers. Now we were really going to learn to March, QCS style. We spent a week constantly marching between blue dots on the parade square, whilst veterans of the QCS either held their heads in despair or guffawed themselves into a near coma. The blue dots represented the layout of the Royal Albert Hall. We had also been informed that our 'bulled' shoes were basically shit and spent hours hopelessly trying to get them to the standard of the guys in the QCS, we had no hope. I consoled myself with the knowledge that we had only just been taught that eliminating 'shine' was a camouflage technique, although I am pretty sure that only meant when we were in the field. One of the great things about RAF Uxbridge is that we were allowed to go off camp every night, up to then we had been incarcerated in RAF Swinderby with only the odd weekend pass towards the end on our training.

The QCS guys told us which pub to go to, so we got changed went to the local 'RAF boozer' marched into the bar ordered beer and were ID'd by the barman it was a complete set up. A couple of us were asked if we wanted to go to Soho by a couple of QCS guys so we jumped at the chance and travelled to Soho after a couple of drinks we were asked if we wanted to watch some porn, silly question of course we did, so our guide and his oppo stated that they would get us in if we paid for them . . . . not a problem. We gained entry to a dubious small cinema bought bottles of beer at extortionate prices and settled down to watch the film. Just as the male actor started getting his leading ladies kit off the QCS guy beside me whispered my name, as I turned to him he poked me in both eyes I couldn't see a thing, they thought it was nearly as hilarious as the fact that they had also told the cinema staff I was under eighteen years of age, I was now on the street in Soho with streaming eyes and my lasting memory? The background music to the film was the same tune they used on TV show Sale of the Century. I'd get the RAF regiment back later in my RAF career.

Attending the Royal Albert Hall is a sombre occasion and to represent your unit or service is a great honour the event went off without incident due to the huge amount of practise we had completed. My Grandparents were able to see me on TV which made them proud as they had never seen me in uniform. I also got to sleep with a Royal Navy Nurse who had appeared on the front of a Queen Alexandra's Royal Naval Nursing Service recruiting pamphlet. Apparently I looked smart but was marching with my mouth open, Mum, Dad and my sister were very, very proud, as was I. Immediately following the event I was sent with 5 other recruits to RAF Mountbatten in Plymouth to undergo my Motor Boat Crewman (MBC) trade training. RAF Mountbatten was a spectacular piece of real estate, a small, peninsular that stretched into Plymouth Sound with one access road, it was not surprising that in later years it was developed and provided luxury accommodation and a marina for those who could afford such lifestyles, I remember thinking on many occasions that Billy Butlin should have bought it.

CHAPTER 5

RAF Mountbatten, First time round

We arrived at RAF Mountbatten on a cold November night after a 30-45 minute journey, on the number 7 bus from Plymouth train station, like 5 Nepalese Sherpa's, we had carried everything with us, we were given 'transit' accommodation, shown were the dining hall was and told to report to the Marine Dock at 08:00. 'Transit' accommodation is basic to say the least and if you are not aware that there is a difference between 'transit' and 'permanent' accommodation you want to go home.

I wanted to go home, I had seen the accommodation that the QCS had been given and this was shit, maybe if I practised marching I could get either transferred to the QCS or at the very least get a better room. I knew the military took marching serious but to base the standard of your accommodation on your ability to bull boots, iron uniform and swing your arms and legs in time seemed a bit extreme. With such strange thoughts racing through my head, I fell asleep. The following morning we duly reported to the Marine Dock to be told we were in the wrong place and had 5 minutes to get to the training school. Within minutes of arriving at the Training Centre I was summoned into the office, what the hell had I done? The admin Corporal asked me:

"Are you 665 Thompson?"

"Yes, why", I replied, after reminding me it was not my place to ask questions he asked:

"Will you volunteer to do duties on camp over the Christmas holidays?" I thought no way and answered:

"I can't Corporal I'm on leave" I said, his reply was abrupt.

"Its cancelled you're not allowed to go home to paddy land, the bastards will kill you, so if you're staying on camp you might as well be on duty"

Fucking IRA, I thought, and then volunteered to do the duties, I couldn't refuse.

Although it was not a wind up I was to find out very quickly that those within the RAF Marine Craft Units (MCUs) were very much practical jokers and that sarcasm reigned supreme. We arrived at the training school, which was a small building beside the Medical Centre and were greeted by an MCU 'legend', Sergeant Harry Duncan which was interesting because one of my fellow recruits was also called Harry Duncan. A lad from Turrock in Scotland and as Scottish as they come, still to this day he is a member of the Tartan Army and an ambassador for everything Scottish. Harry would get drunk and recite to the tune of 'Oh Christmas Tree' 'Oh Hogmanay, Oh Hogmanay, only??? days to Hogmanay', this was ok but Harry would start singing this from January 2nd so the countdown began at 'only 364 days to Hogmanay'. We were then taken to the Station stores and issued with our MBC equipment. This consisted of sea boots (wellies), long white woolly socks, a white 'woolly pully' jumper, No 8 boots, two No 8 shirts, two pairs of No 8 trousers and green foul weather gear. MCU personnel wore the same working dress as Royal Navy personnel i.e. dark blue shirts and trousers instead of the normal RAF light blue shirts and grey trousers, we were after all training to become the RAFs sailors, the only thing on our working dress that was really RAF was the beret and cap badge. MBC trade training would take 10 weeks throughout that time we would learn Morse code by Aldis lamp, bends and hitches, splicing wire and rope, seamanship skills and sea survival skills. As a new intake we were to be known as 'Baby Boaties', it kept you in your place in the NAFFI bar at night and guaranteed you would get your fair share of 'shitty jobs' whilst training to become a real boatie. We were devastated to find out very quickly that helicopters were now the at the forefront of the RAF Search and Rescue (SAR) force, and the MCUs role would, over time, diminish, but we still had a vital role to play. Shortly after our dreams had been shattered we were informed that the following day we were being sent to RAF Catterick the home of RAF Regiment trade training.

This wasn't because we had our trades had altered or because we needed further training to deal with the communist hordes. The Fire Brigades Union had balloted its members and they had voted in favour of a National strike, we were being sent to RAF Catterick as it was also the base for training RAF fire fighters and so two weeks of intensive fire fighting training was undertaken. The Baby Boaties fighting alongside the established crews, not just fires but during training with some of the other units that were based and training there also. Told you I'd get the RAF regiment back. Boarding school had paid off!

After two weeks intensive training I was despatched to Wigan and bedded down in a local Territorial Army Centre for the duration of the strike. The people of Wigan welcomed us with open arms and although we were certainly no match for the professional fire fighters that had gone on strike we didn't lose anyone. That said we did inadvertently cause some damage to property due to a lack of knowledge and skills.

I recall one 'shout' were the locals had tried to help by lifting a fire hydrant cover prior to our arrival; the Green Goddess screeched to a halt and as the crew jumped out one of them went straight into the hydrant housing and broke his ankle. On another occasion I was told by a colleague to pull down the guttering on a terraced house as it was posing a danger to those attempting to put out a fire in the house. I reached up with a large 'boat hook' type instrument and pulled, nothing, those Victorians knew how to put up guttering, none of your PVC shit here. After a period of time swinging like a pendulum, achieving nothing and starting to become the focus of attention for the ever increasing crowd I summoned help from a colleague and for a while we both swung on the implement to no avail, much to the amusement of the crowd. Right one last bloody huge tug should do it, synchronised like Olympic trampolinists we jumped in tandem and grabbed the 'boathook' device, to my horror in what appeared to be slow motion the cast iron guttering of the whole terraced block, around 20 houses crashed to the ground, the gathered crowd clapped and cheered. Sheepishly we made ourselves anonymous.

A fire in a paper mill required every Green Goddess from our base to be sent, to us this was the 'big one', we had endured stories from retained fire fighters, who were not on strike, "that you've never been to a real fire until you've been to one with 10 pumps", yes we had! I ended up manning a hose with one other airman and we foolishly went further into the building than we should have, but my colleague, who was considerably older than me, was constantly telling me "we'll get a medal for this son", posthumously I thought. Suddenly out of the smoke appeared a bright light, I thought I had died and this was my calling from above, I apologised to God for stealing four Black Jacks from a sweet shop when I was 9, but mitigated the crime by saying a big boy made me do it and also apologised for telling the Policeman lies in Tywyn. I said goodbye to my family and wondered what heaven would be like? Then a bloody forklift with a burning bale of paper and a lunatic of airman on it came hurtling towards us, there goes the medal I thought but hey I'm still alive, the forklift then skidded when trying to avoid us and dropped the burning bale of paper which partially blocked a door behind us and set fire to more paper bales which had until this time survived, I am dead now I thought. At this point the lunatic from the forklift and my colleague decided to argue over who was in the wrong, I was left struggling to control a fire hose that had now adopted the characteristics of a scalded python, it was writhing all over the place and I was weakening rapidly and starting to slide on the wet floor, I really am dead now I thought. My comrades decided that they would adjourn until a later time and date and helped me get the every strengthening 'python' under control, your both dead when we get out of here I thought. Between the three of us we extinguished the burning bales that were blocking our exit and made our escape. Once outside we were asked to give a SITREP (situation report) on our foolhardy actions once that was done the ensuing argument resumed, this time with fists involved and the public watching, it was surreal.

Part of the cause was that the RAF had not given us High Visibility clothing they had provided us with the British Forces standard Disruptive Pattern Material (DPM) camouflage clothing, that was clever wasn't it. Let's give them two weeks training, fire engines from the early fifties, give them clothing which is meant to help them become invisible and send them into dark burning buildings, often at night. The building wasn't a total loss but the contents were.

As the strike continued we became more competent at responding to and dealing with fires, but the children of Wigan knew how to make us look foolish at one garage fire three Green Goddesses arrived the crews quickly and adeptly set up the appropriate equipment got ready to open the garage door in full view of a crowd of teenagers the garage was open and we found a small pile of burning foam which had produced masses of smoke, we looked like pillocks. At another fire several Green Goddesses from the RAF were dealing with a house fire when the Royal Navy 'Flying Squad' arrived to assist, they didn't receive a warm welcome they had parked on the hoses of the RAF and those at the face of the fire were now endeavouring to 'flick' dribbles of water onto a burning building. The Navy Goddess soon moved. At a chimney fire the responding Green Goddess screeched to a halt and ejaculated its crew, who climbed on the roof and promptly put their hose down the chimney and turned the water on, one very dirty carpet and living room I think. The name 'Flying Squad' was what an RN team had named one of their Green Goddess, most service teams named their Goddesses, ours was the "Dirty Half Dozen" due to the fact that there was a crew of six on each vehicle. At one point some wag stuck a coal board marketing poster on the side of a Green Goddess, it was quickly removed as the strap line of the market campaign was "Come home to a real fire", funny, but not appropriate. I am sure that all the servicemen and women that took part in that strike cover and all future strikes have similar tales to tell, one that will go down in infamy was of a crew who had rescued a cat from a tree, gratefully accepted tea and buns from the elderly owner as a reward, and then promptly ran over the cat, killing it, when departing back to base. The gentle folk of Wigan were grateful for us being there and the free pints in pubs and clubs for the servicemen were welcomed, as was the attention of the local girls; however I bet they were relieved when the professionals came back to work. I know this experience made me realise what a difficult job fire-fighters have and how highly skilled they are.

Following the strike we returned to being Baby Boaties and resumed our trade training. The food had improved in quality as RAF Mountbatten was an operational station but the quantity was still questionable. The good folk at NAAFI provide the usual mini market were rations could be supplemented and they also provided a facility called an AUTOMAT. In short this was a room full of vending machines that provided the usual products such as sandwiches, pies, chocolate and drinks. These machines dispensed crisps and chocolate bars which were held in rows and when the appropriate 'code' was entered the row rotated and the product fell to a bin at the base of the machine and the buyer simply grabbed their chosen delight and consumed it. The prices were astronomical, but with their usual resolve marine craft crews found a cheaper way of getting the stuff out of one particular machine! The secret was a cat!! If you placed a cat in the bin at the base of the machine it duly became frightened and tried to extricate itself the result being that it would knock off produce into the retrieval bin, free stuff. After a while the cat would be released. Throughout this training we really didn't get much 'sea time' apart from learning how to receive and respond to helm orders, taking a small craft alongside a bigger vessel, that was it, this would be 'experiential learning' when we became crew. We continued every day to learn Morse code, by lamp, and to throw a heaving line accurately. However after 10 weeks we were no longer Baby Boaties we had passed our trade training and another group had now adopted that nomenclature. We were given our postings I was to stay at RAF Mountbatten with another two newly qualified Boaties and two of our colleagues were posted to RAF Alness, in Scotland.

CHAPTER 6

Joining a Marine Craft Unit

The Marine Dock was the epicentre of Marine Craft Operations it was the dock that boats would come into to load fuel, fresh water, stores and any additional passengers. This is where, every morning, the unit would parade to ensure everyone was present before departing on small ferry boats, called marine tenders or MT boats for short, for their respective vessels. It was also the home of "Bat Marine", the dock office. It was this small single story, three roomed building that acted as our port operations centre and where we all carried out our 24 hour guard duties. I remember coming down to the dock one day to see nearly the whole squadron peering over the railings and looking into the actual dock, all I could see was a couple of small blue fenders.

I enquired "What's wrong" to be snarled at "Can't you see those blue fenders?"

I replied "Yes"

"Well the fucking MT boat is attached to them"

Oh shit, I could feel a Courts Martial coming on for the duty watch who had fallen asleep, forgot to check the lines on the MT boat, which at low water had become snagged. As the tide rose the MT Boat didn't, the fenders did though. It wasn't just that, every vessel in the Squadron had been left unchecked all night, anything could have happened. They could have been stolen by the communist hordes. The day after our Motor Boat Crew training finished I reported to the Marine Dock at RAF Mountbatten to be allocated to a boat, that morning I was told to clean out a fuel bunker and take mail to and from the Station HQ, I never got near a bloody boat. These supernumerary tasks continued for around a week, any shitty job that came into the Squadron was given to the 'new guys'.

The first boat I was assigned to was a Rescue Target Towing Launch Mark 2 or RTTL for short. It was beautiful, constructed from double diagonal oak planks, she was 68 foot long and powered by two Sea Griffin engines, these were converted Spitfire engines, and these vessels ran on aviation fuel and had to be started with a cartridge. They were beasts; they could hit forty knots when conditions were right. The RAF were only allowed to use the nomenclature Her Majesty's Air Force Vessel (HMAFV) for vessels over 68 feet, anything of 68 Foot and under were given numbers. She was 2757 and I would only serve on her for a very short time as she was destined to go on display at the Royal Air Force museum Hendon, where she resides to this day. The daily routine for crews would be to take a small 'transit ferry' from the marine dock to your vessel the first task of the day was to 'scrub down', this basically meant that you washed your boat and got rid of the seagull shit that they were covered in each night. Then if not sailing, general vessel maintenance was undertaken, painting, wire brushing, greasing etc. The boats fulfilled many tasks as varied as acting a winching platforms for RAF helicopter crews to practice, towing targets for both aircraft and the shore based guns of HMS Cambridge the RN gunnery school, to training Aircrew in sea survival skills (RAF

Mountbatten was also home to the RAF School of Combat Survival), range safety patrols and a task named Operation Grenada. The latter was a shared operation with the RN and was a patrol off the Northern Ireland coast to deter and detect gun running by the paramilitaries. All of these tasks had their benefits and I have to say hazards. If you were to sail then you still had to 'scrub down' whilst 'in transit', there was a technique behind this. We would normally use buckets with rope attached to the handle to gather sea water to "scrub down' and if you were underway the trick was to dangle the bucket over the side of the boat by the engine cooling outlets and fill the buckets that way. I remember going reasonably slow across Plymouth Sound and a new deckhand being told to put the bucket over the side to get water, as the coxswain started to open up the engine the deckhand launched his tethered bucket into the sea and was violently ripped off the deck as the bucket had become an anchor and the only thing that was going to give was his balance. He never did that again. Nowadays it would be promulgated as lessons learned and have to be reported to the HSE under RIDDOR, we just kept quiet and enjoyed the beer it brought us as a result of keeping quiet. As always the RAF was part of a Government review and the cost of running the RTTL mark 2s was deemed uneconomical, so the RAF decide to withdraw them, 2757 was to become an exhibit at the RAF museum in Hendon, yes a trip to London. We took 2757 to London, stripped her of all her essential equipment and watched as she was lifted out of the water, placed on a trailer and taken to Hendon, we had some time to tidy her up and then sadly said our goodbyes, all mariners end up with an infinity with their craft, this did not appear to be the dignified end that this magnificent specimen of marine architecture, design and engineering deserved.

I was soon part of an RAF 'Pinnace' crew. These were again numbered I was on 1390, due to their length, again double diagonal timber plank built boats, they had a small wheel-house, crew quarters, galley, heads (toilet), radio office and a large cargo compartment towards the stern.

These primarily worked alongside staff at the sea survival school. Undertaking the sea survival task was great and allowed the practical jokers to shine. Sometimes crew members waited until the aircrew had boarded to boat and as we departed Plymouth Sound one crew member would rapidly appear on deck with a sick bag retching and pretending to be sick. The on looking aircrew were unaware that the bag contained cold vegetable soup the look on their faces when the boat crew suddenly dug into the contents of the bag with spoons was a picture. This trick worked particularly well when the weather was rough and the aircrew were using every sinew to hold down the contents of their stomachs, often they failed. Of course when they departed the boats for their individual survival dinghies we would monitor their progress to ensure they safely got into this vital piece of equipment, if the weather wasn't rough we made it rough by making fast passes very close to the dinghies, our aim was to capsize as many as possible. The Health and Safety Executive would have had a fit. This was great, in the armed forces and able to 'knock it up' officers! As soon as the aircrew had been deposited in their life rafts out came the fishing rods, the RAF boat crews always carried their fishing rods and always retuned from such tasks with at least a bucket full of Mackerel.

On another occasion I was 'volunteered' and ended up in a 24 man life raft with two other airmen as part of a training expedition for a Nimrod aircraft, we were to assist the aircrew in practising 'Lindholme drops'. This was a survival pack that dropped from an aircraft to assist downed airmen or ships crews. The gear consisted of between three and five fibreglass canisters, the centre one was the largest and contained a spare life raft that would automatically inflate upon impact with the sea. The remaining two to four canisters contain food, water, clothing and communications equipment and the whole lot were joined by floating orange line. It was a fine summers day off Devon and we thought we had got ourselves a bit of a skive by volunteering for this exercise; I couldn't understand why there were so few volunteers. The idea was that once the responding aircraft had spotted us they would reduce altitude, calculate wind and tidal drift and deposit the Lindholme gear up tide so it drifted towards the grateful survivor, that's the theory. We were given the signal to let off orange smoke markers to help the aircraft, this we did, the aircraft could be seen to reduce height and then conducted a dummy run, and you may imagine the expletives and reactions of the three of us in the dinghy when the Lindholme gear exited the aircraft. The gear deployed perfectly but appeared to be plummeting directly towards the dinghy. Anyone that has completed a sea survival course will appreciate how difficult it can be to get into such contraptions; I can assure you getting out is really easy, the three of us leapt into the sea off our safe haven. The canisters missed the life raft but the floating line actually lay across the life raft, they had obviously been practising bombing the communist hordes. I wondered if these guys had recently completed a course at the survival school and this was actually an act of revenge.

I was then transferred to HMAFV Sea Otter, this was another steel built boat and was 120 feet in length, there were three in the class the other two being Seal and Seagull and both were based at Alness in Scotland. Their official name was Long Range Recovery and Support Vessels or LRRSVs for short. The steel RAF boats were renowned for their bad sea keeping capabilities and the LRRSVs were the worst, it was often said that they had more rocking and rolling than Elvis, I can confirm this I got sea sick nearly every day aboard Sea Otter, but I loved it. On one particular trip I was actually at the helm with a bucket beside me so I wasn't sick on the wheelhouse floor. These were the largest boats in the RAF fleet and had a crew of 17 consisting of two Officers, 3 NCOs and 12 Airmen, as for stability they had none, they were bastards, but they did have a bar on board. In reality it was a cupboard with a beer pump in it there was no choice of beverage at this bar. As to be expected the crew accommodation was the best in the fleet with the crew actually getting proper bunks and in comparison to the other vessels in the fleet the galley was huge and we had a cook to boot. It was these vessels that undertook the Operation Grenade patrols in support of Operation Banner (the overall code name for the Northern Ireland Campaign). It was during one of these operations that I was able to finally get my long disappointed father onto an RAF boat. We arrived at Airport Wharf in Belfast, this was patrolled by Royal Navy personnel and was the 'secure berth' for visiting warships, I couldn't tell my Father when or what time we were arriving, as I didn't know, but as he was still in the Army and 'working' in Northern Ireland he was able to use his contacts to find out. He pulled up at the gate to the Wharf and as he wound his car window down and said "hello" a skinny Matelot nervously pushed the business end of an SLR through the window. This was understandable here was a civilian car with an rugged looking gent who spoke with a broad Belfast accent, not the best credentials for visiting your son in a war zone but it was adequate for the work the Queen had wanted him to do, remember that cunning in Aden? The sailor was obviously scared and my Father recalls him physically shaking, so to ease the mind of the poor Matelot and defuse the situation my Father opened his civilian coat exposed his issue firearm and told the sailor "Army, now get that fucking weapon out of my face or I'll shoot you", good call Dad! Once another sailor checked my father's ID card and consoled his gibbering mate my father was granted access to the jetty we were berthed on.

The Duty lookout called me to the flying bridge and my Father came aboard. I tried to give my father the heads up about the First Officer, who was a bit of a hygiene freak, but I didn't get a chance the First Officer appeared on the Flying Bridge and introduced himself, my Father returned the introduction and stuck out his hand, I cringed. The First Officer paused then eventually with apprehension shook hands with my Dad and upon completion of that international gesture of friendship and peace extracted a handkerchief from his pocket and wiped his hand, I knew what was coming.

"Sir, with all due respect what the fuck is that all about", my Dad asked.

"Germs" the reply was short.

"Listen Sir, if you ever do that to me again it will not be germs that kill you, it will be fucking me" he was always one to acknowledge rank!

The First Officer scurried away, undoubtedly to have a shower. As my Father and I went below the coxswain of the boat, who was generally unpopular informed me of the following "As your Father is a senior rank take him into the Senior Ranks Mess to get a beer", my mistake I didn't listen. It was my Father that was allowed in the Senior Ranks Mess, I WASN'T, Dad politely refused the kind offer at the same time as being able to murmur "wanker" under his breath and came into the Junior Ranks mess with me and we opened the cupboard. I know they say in small communities news travels fast, it's true I have seen it for real, in the time it had taken my Dad to meet two pricks and transit his way to my mess he had become a legend. After a few beers he left, convinced the RAF were strange. Apparently the Navy Guard at the main gate said sorry as my Father departed! These patrols normally went on for between 20-30 days and to this day I'm not sure what they contributed to the fight against domestic terrorism.

In the middle of these patrols we were granted a period of rest and recuperation simply known as R&R in exotic places such as the Port Ellen on the island of Islay or Stornoway on the Isle of Lewis. These 3-4 day breaks not only gave us the chance to take on fresh water and supplies but allowed the crew to spend some of their hard earned cash on getting out of their heads on alcohol but also attempt to get into the knickers of anything female, it was a case of quantity and not quality! Some of those ladies were very grateful. It was not unknown for crew members to be seen getting out of taxis or being dropped off with minutes to spare every morning, after nights of passion with the locals. On one occasion in Stornoway a star of a highly popular Saturday TV show was hosting a disco at the local RAF camp so we determined that that's where all the local ladies would be going and we attempted to get in, but we didn't have tickets. The entire spare fanny on the island was in the one place and we were not allowed in, it was time for some of that Thompson family cunning to come into play!!! Myself and Phil (another crew member) decided that we would tell the RAF guard that we were from the RAF News and were there to interview the star, daft buggers let us in and we ended up having beer and bickies with the host. The Saturday morning TV show was Swap Shop and the host was none other than Noel Edmunds, I can honestly say he runs a good "Green Room".

Although not as exotic or as bloody warm as many other places I had and have since been to, Port Ellen and Stornoway are places which hold fond memories for me. Little did I know at the time that I would, in the future, visit Port Ellen on numerous occasions, wearing another uniform.

CHAPTER 7

Tenby and beyond

My next posting was to Tenby in South Wales, I never realised at the time that this posting would have such a significant impact on my life and future. It was a small detachment consisting of a Warrant Officer in charge, a mechanic, a cook and 9 other personnel who operated the 68ft Pinnace 1388 that was located there.

The Officer in charge was a Warrant Officer who was from Sandy Row, in Northern Ireland and he was heading towards retirement, his first bit of advice to me upon arriving at the unit was to 'leave my daughters alone, they don't date ugly people', I didn't even know he had daughters. I was soon to find out he was a Marine Craft legend. His wife told me in later years that, when courting, he told her was from the capital of Ireland where they played 'tig' with hatchets! The accommodation for the single personnel was a former public toilet and cafe block which sat on the pier at Tenby, the main function of this detachment was to ensure range safety for Pendine Ranges, to provide a platform for equipment which boffins wanted to test at sea and as ever to provide a practise platform for the rescue helicopter crews based at RAF Brawdy.

Tenby was a gift of a posting every day we would launch our rubber 'Gemini' and go out to the boat, scrub down and if there was no tasking, sit there and listen to radio 1 and 'Our tune' with Dave Lee Travis! If the tide was in then the Gemini would be launched using a crane at the end of the pier, nice and easy, however if the tide was out we would have to take the Gemini to the tide line on a trailer and launch from the beach. If the weather blew up this became a challenge and was a case of wading out past the surf line with the Gemini in tow and all leaping in, again if the HSE had of known it the RAF would have been in the shit. Crew members were regularly flung out of the Gemini during this process. One unusual element of being stationed at Tenby was that if Southeasterly gale force 8 was forecast we would crew up (night or day) and head for a bay off Caldey Island for refuge as the regular moorings were very exposed. The one single benefit of a small unit is that you can keep secrets. We had a small fibreglass rowing boat at Tenby and we would use this at weekends to go fishing. It was powered by a tiny Seagull 5HP engine and was official military equipment as it was on the detachment inventory. The rubber Gemini tenders that we would normally use to transit to the Pinnace had been vandalised and were inoperable so we were ordered to use this tender as a means of transport until they had been replaced. One day I was tasked with taking the Coxswain ashore and duly embarked upon the dinghy and started the engine, the Coxswain embarked and we proceeded towards Tenby harbour, on the way one of the local fishermen (we'll call him Dai) decided to play 'chicken' with the dinghy. He however misjudged and rammed the dinghy, cut it in half and it duly sank depositing myself and the Coxswain into the water. We both sunk like stone due to the fact we were wearing sea boots (wellies) both of us 'banged off' our lifejackets and then shot to the surface, the first words the Coxswain said to me were 'You're in the shit for this and Sammy (the Warrant Officer in Charge) is going to kill you', not a mention regarding my welfare! The fisherman recovered us and took us back to the pier, Sammy was as to be expected a bit pissed off, but that was it, no report to the RAF no report to the Marine Accident Investigation Board (MAIB), we just kept the secret and the fisherman got off scott free and Sammy probably got free fish and beer for months.

I ended up with every shitty job at the site until someone else became the focus of Sammy's attention, given that this was Tenby that wasn't too long I won't go into detail but can I take this opportunity to thank Dizzy!!!!

We also had a request to assist with the spreading of the ashes, at sea, of an RAF veteran. We scrubbed and polished the boat ready to receive the family of the deceased, the boat was brought alongside in Tenby harbour and the crew donned their Number 1s or dress uniform. The family group arrived, around 9 persons, and we duly sailed out to sea, as you may imagine the day was quite sombre. We reached the designated place and the family's minister delivered a moving speech of how the veteran had served in the latter years of the Second World War and in numerous campaigns thereafter. The tears of the widow and the other family members began to flow as soon as a bugler from RAF Brawdy played the last post. The boat and main family members had been positioned so as to ensure that the ashes would follow the wind and blow away from the boat, imagine our horror when, in a split second, the urn was passed to what appeared to be a Granddaughter at the back of the main group and she immediately launched the ashes into wind! They duly blew back all over the smartly dressed airmen and the now howling family. Best we get back to Tenby . . . . sharpish. We disembarked the now arguing family and laid the rest of the veteran airman to rest by using hoses to wash down the decks!!! In reality that meant that half of the poor sod had been buried out at sea and the other half in Tenby Harbour, we were dignified though; we waited until the family had departed before starting to wash down. Our mechanic would regularly use RAF time, equipment and material to provide a service to the local mariners, the Officer in Charge would also help out locals by preparing and laying moorings. Hearts and minds I told myself. It was alleged that one 'old and bold' deckhand and a well connected RAF mechanic even sold ex RAF lifejackets and other equipment to local boat crews!! The MOD would have cringed if they knew exactly what had gone on a Tenby. This detachment had always been popular with RAF crews and it was easy to see why, none of the rigid discipline of a large RAF base, but all the benefits.

It was 1980 and I had met a young woman, who was working as a waitress/chambermaid in a local hotel. I had actually spilt a drink over her white dress in Cinderella's disco and went back the next day to offer to pay for it to get cleaned and decided to ask her out. You know the saying 'young, dumb and full of cum'. Any way she said yes and to cut a long story short we ended up engaged and eventually married after a short period. There wasn't such an emphasis on Health and Safety as there is nowadays and I remember five days before my wedding I ended up falling overboard onto a mooring buoy, landing with one leg in the water and one leg on the buoy the boat gently lowered herself in the water touched my back and sent my testicles shooting up behind my ears. There was no bloody RIDDOR report went in for that. The RAF only had a limited number of married quarters at a place called Manobier and there were no spare houses, so we ended up in a bedsit, until the RAF were able to negotiate with HM Coastguard to use one of the spare Coastguard houses in Tenby. Again I didn't know what an impact this or the regular chats with my new neighbour would have on my future and the fact that I would visit this house on several occasions throughout a different career.

Anyone who has lived in married quarters will know that you are not allowed to officially decorate to your own taste, it is normally neutral colours such as Magnolia throughout, and the one huge benefit for a newly married couple is that they are completely furnished. I was called to the house with a very snooty RAF Families Officer from RAF Brawdy to check the inventory and sign for my new married quarter. Being an ex Coastguard house it was furnished to a higher standard that the normal married quarter and the colour scheme was different to say the least, the bathroom was bright orange, but it had a shower! The Families Officer was disgusted that a junior rank had an orange bathroom with a shower and fitted carpets in every room, so he ordered that the shower was removed, the bathroom be painted Magnolia and all the fitted carpets were removed and replaced with normal Junior ranks carpets!!!! One night In November 1981 whilst lying in bed my pregnant wife informed me she thought her waters were about to break, I immediately went into 'married quarter' mode and pushed her out of the bed so she wouldn't stain the mattress and herded her into the bathroom so she wouldn't stain the bedroom carpet, you get fined for stains on things when you vacate a married quarter!

As I couldn't drive at the time we called an ambulance and eventually my son was born at Haverfordwest Hospital, about 25 miles from Tenby. I was wholly unprepared for the return journey and was wearing trousers, a jumper and slippers this was November and it was hammering it down with sleet. I had no money and had to get home, so I started walking, after about an hour a Police car pulled up alongside me and asked me why I was out in the early hours of the morning dressed as I was, I told the Police Officer of my adventure he congratulated me and told me I was going the wrong way, gave me directions and then drove off, I have never had a place in my heart for Dyfed, Powys Police since then. I eventually thumbed lifts from the very few vehicles that were around and got back to Tenby at 09:30, got washed, shaved into uniform and into work . . . . Sammy bollocked me for being late. The forces are desperate to protect their reputation and rightly so, however there can be occasions when the great British public can stick their noses in where it really shouldn't be and they will often not realise the consequences of their actions. Following the birth of my son my then Father in law and I went out to wet the baby's head, accompanied by most of the RAF Tenby detachment, I got absolutely hammered and when going home I had to crawl from the taxi to my front door, one of my neighbours complained and I got charged with bringing the service into disrepute and fined £50.

I remember another occasion when I was on duty at Tenby and the a young police officer called in for a cup of tea and a bacon butty in the early hours of the morning, which wasn't unknown, the cop was enjoying the warm hospitality of the unit when his radio cackled into life reporting strange lights in the harbour. Both him and I went out to look for the reported lights and low and behold part of the harbour was periodically lighting up an dull orange colour, we couldn't for the life of us work out what it was, but he had me convinced it was something weird to do with the Military Research Facility at Pendine Ranges near Saundersfoot. So he called in the CID to assist as it was beginning to rain we went back into the RAF unit to await the arrival of the Detectives and between us we had discussed and discounted aliens, lightening and the communist hordes. CID arrived within about 15 minutes by which time the flashing lights had now spread to right across the harbour and were getting closer to the RAF side, maybe it was the communist hordes? We explained that the situation has worsened in the 15 minutes since the Police Officer had submitted his report. Still perplexed one of the boys from the unit was returning from town, somewhat the worse for wear and announced the answer to the Police Officers and I. He had been walking back and had decided to throw all the yellow roadside hazard warning lights into the harbour. At the time he thought this was a great laugh, I'm not sure whether he thought it was worth the £60 fine the court imposed though.

After two years at Tenby I was posted back to RAF Mountbatten, a disappointment but orders are orders!

CHAPTER 8

Back to 'Batten

Returning to RAF Mountbatten was totally different for me, I was now married and had a young son, unfortunately there were no married quarters available so the RAF 'sorted me' out with a caravan at Fort Stamford Holiday village just outside the camp. It was a shit hole, but I had to go on the waiting list to get a house on one of the 'married patches'. The forces are paranoid about servicemen and women getting into debt, this goes all the way back to the cold war when such individuals were seen as vulnerable to corruption or influence by the communist hordes and open to exploitation by the then opposition. In simple terms if they get into debt they can be easily coerced into passing state secrets to the enemy, financial history is still considered nowadays when individuals are being security vetted! One particular Corporal at RAF Mountbatten was in serious shit for bouncing cheques and was duly charged and fined he asked if he could pay the resultant fine by cheque and was told yes, guess what happened? . . . . you've got it, the cheque bounced and he was whisked off to military detention. He was also told he would lose his married quarter as a result of this latest indiscretion, although sad for him I was overjoyed as I was near the top of the housing list. Unfortunately when the married quarter was inspected upon his family vacating it, some of the furniture and a number of doors had been burnt to keep them warm! The communist hordes wouldn't have needed money they could have blackmailed him with coal! As a result this quarter became unavailable and I had to wait another 3 months for a house. This put an added strain on my beginning to struggle marriage, from which it would never recover.

I was then moved onto another type of vessel the Rescue Target Towing Launch (RTTL) mark 3, these were steel built RAF Vessels. This class of boat had identifying numbers but because they were over the requisite 68 foot, they were also given names such as Lancaster, Halifax, Spitfire, Hurricane, Sunderland and the last of the class Wellington. It was Wellington that I joined, although nearly 30 years since I served on her I still remember her official radio call sign 2VLX. These vessels were palatial compared to the wooden boats, but they were nowhere near as 'romantic'. The primary task of these vessels was target towing. Leaving Plymouth Sound one day on such a task we 'streamed' an object called a Delta target, this was constructed from two pontoons connected by a steel lattice work and topped by two bright orange RADAR reflectors, these were towed up to a mile behind the towing vessel. The vessel would transit 'legs' and Royal Navy gunners training at HMC Cambridge would endeavour to track the and fire at the target.

The aim was not to hit the target, it was to fire short and long in a straddle pattern. One day I was on the boat undertaking this task and all went well until the Navy started firing, the first two shots straddled the towing boat, very quickly the wireless operator (WOP) informed the Navy that on this occasion we were "towing the target, not fucking pushing it", the firing stopped, the gunners re-calibrated and we carried on. This wouldn't be the last time I came under 'friendly fire'. The WOP got a bollocking for swearing on the radio! That didn't worried him for in general terms the WOPs were the marine crafts nutters equal only to the marine fitters, it must have been all the white noise and oil.

An additional benefit of crewing a RTTL Mark 3 was that you got to go away to exotic places like Lowestoft and Great Yarmouth, for many crews these towns became second homes and certain bed and breakfast establishments made a reasonable living from the RAF crews, as they didn't live on board when on such detachments, they were on what the RAF called 'rate ones', this was an extra £16 per day. This was an overnight subsistence rate and provided accommodation, a little food and lots of beer, but not in that order. Most crews stayed in the same B&B and they got to know the landladies quite well. One morning I got up in our chosen B&B, and the carpet of the room I shared was soaking my colleague quickly established that the kettle had leaked, the landlady was so apologetic for letting her boys down, she gave us a larger than usual breakfast and the night for free, it was only later that he confessed to trying to piss in the sink after a night on the pop, he missed. On a positive note, and I always try to find positive in everything no matter how hard, he missed and I had washed and brushed my teeth in that sink. Yarmouth was a great run ashore for the RAF crews and many of the local establishments welcomed us like sons coming home whenever we turned up. As to be expected there were a number of locals who became genuine friends of crew members. In later years a number of RAF crews would move to the area to crew the very same boats for various civilian operators, doing exactly what they had done as servicemen. Hey same job but with union membership and overtime thrown in.

From time to time we would take part in exercises with the Royal Navy and other NATO forces, we always got cast as Warsaw Pact fast patrol boats, even though the real things were much faster than our boats. It was because of this that we had to use guile and cunning or in layman's terms cheat. I remember hiding, not me personally, but the boat behind the Mew Stone, which was a large rock outside Plymouth Sound, we waited in ambush for our victim. As HMS whatever her name was departing Plymouth we cranked the boat up to full speed shot out from our lair, whipped in behind the ship and fired off two green very flares. These were flares that were fired from a cartridge gun and came in a range of hues red, green, white and illumination flares. Anyway we had killed or at least disabled our target, we were the communist hordes!

Triumphantly we celebrated with hot beverages and the staple diet of all RAF boats crews 'egg banjos' or fried egg sandwiches to the uninitiated. Suddenly the WOP reported a Morse code signal from a very disgruntled Naval Officer stating:

"Unfair, what were you doing in that minefield" as the RAF vessels Captain thought of a response the WOP stated:

"It's alright boss, I've replied", the skipper looked somewhat shocked then asked:

"What did you say?" the WOP then replied:

"32 fucking knots".

Yes it was the very same WOP that had been told off previously for swearing at the Navy, very soon after the exercise he was transferred to another boat.

At the time the Army also operated this class of vessel. These were in the custody of the Royal Corps of Transport and were named after winners of the Victoria Cross. One such vessel the Michael Murphy

VC visited RAF Mountbatten and for a time was moored alongside one of our boats, the army obviously were grateful for our assistance in providing them with some refuge and rations. However I wonder how they felt when the eventually found out that RAF crews had painted yellow daisies on her under the 'flare' of the bow. This ensured that the crew couldn't see the new adornments whilst on board, but everyone else could. I am sure they thought well of the crowd of RAF personnel waving them off when they departed for pastures new, that was until they found the new colour scheme. After 14 months at RAF Mountbatten I returned to living on camp, my marriage was over all but for the paperwork. Returning to the life of a singleton is very easy when you're in the forces as some of your mates rally round to support you, some will even try to get off with your wife! The Lads in my Marine Craft unit did both, thanks guys!

The skipper of HMAFV Wellington started to notice that I was missing targets whilst on lookout and sent me for an eye test and to my total devastation I failed it, I was immediately taken off the crew and assigned a shore side role. I have to say this skipper was one of the best I had ever served with and for a time I hated him after being designated 'unfit for sea service' however with hindsight his decision set the path of my future and for that I'm thankful. I was either tasked with helping out with boats that were undergoing refit or running about doing shitty jobs, enough was enough I wasn't doing this for the rest of my days so I asked to re-muster (RAF speak for changing trades). I was duly processed out of the unit and sent to RAF Innsworth, the RAF Personnel Management Centre. I underwent a series of tests and was scheduled to re-muster to train as an Air Load Master with the intention of progressing to helicopter aircrew. That was until some twat noticed, 4 weeks into my training my eyesight results, so I was sent back to RAF Innisworth. This time despite asking to re-muster to the RAF Regiment I was told they had no vacancies and was offered a stewards job, no way after the joys of RAF Marine Craft Units, becoming a waiter would have killed me, I turned that offer down, twice. I was finally called into a Warrant Officers office to be offered the stewards job again I, once more, declined the offer and was told on the spot:

"Okay go home on leave, your being discharged" that was it, RAF career over; J8136665 Thompson had not only left the building but the service.

CHAPTER 9

Homeward bound

It's December 1984, I'm separated and unemployed . . . . Happy bloody holidays! I'd have applied to join the Ulster Defence Regiment but there were a number of security checks to go through and the usual recruitment paperwork to complete. So I tried to utilise my RAF Marine Craft experiences and having listened to my neighbour in Tenby applied to join HM Coastguard, only to be told by a nice lady that I had all the qualifications and experience required but at 24 I was too young and to 'call back when your 28'.

I then tried to get work breaking into the 'closed shop' of Belfast Pilot boats to be told I was 'over qualified' as a deckhand. So I'm living at home with my parents and my sister the main problem is that my parents only own a two bedroom end terrace house and my bed is the sofa. The house was opposite the local pub so I spent a lot of time in there and through one of my Fathers friends who used the pub, I was offered an interim job as a security guard (at least it was another uniform) at a local industrial site. Nothing too challenging and I had a guard dog! The site was a large and housed a steel fabrication company, Birds Eye foods, and engineering company, some other small businesses and a Radio Rentals depot. Whilst on duty one night conducting a routine patrol of the site I noticed lights and noise coming from the vicinity of the Radio Rentals site so torch held above the head like the movies and the dog in front I set off to investigate. My next memory is waking up beside Radio Rentals with a busting headache and no dog! I then notice blood coming from the back of my head and that the doors to the unit were open and it was empty. Shit. The police were called, arrived interviewed me and asked me where all the TVs and the dog were, I had no idea. The dog was eventually found in Carrickfergus, 7 miles way, three days later, the bugger had either run off or got a lift with the thieves, I never heard a bloody things about the TVs. I had worked there for around eight months and was only being paid £90 per week, not enough to get my head caved in so I left. The UDR informed me that they would prefer me to wait until my divorce was finalised and that I should re-apply once it was all over and done with. In short they didn't want a potentially emotionally unstable (their words not mine) individual running about at work with a firearm and live ammunition or taking home 9mm Browning Personal Protection Weapon (PPW). What now, my solicitor told me my divorce could take up to 2 years to be completed.

I then joined a security company (another uniform) providing security at department stores in Belfast city centre, the most prestigious site was Boots in Royal Avenue and everyone wanted to work there because the female staff were as sexy as hell. The first site I worked at was the Co-Operative department store and within two days I was involved in my first shoplifting incident. The small radio I had cackled and the voice stated that all security guards were to make their way to the exits on my way there a male, around 40 years of age, went flying past me with a handful of jumpers under his arm, initially taken aback I like the other security guards gave chase as he ran into the street, I somehow, ended up at the front of the queue and tried to grab him, he shrugged off this attempt and kept running, I tried to shoulder barge him but missed and knocked over a stall displaying shortbread, the bugger kept on going, but I caught up with him, I grabbed my personal radio by the antenna and swung it like a club at his head he dropped £800 worth of jumpers and hit the floor like a stone . . . . result. NO I had chased him to point near the then 'notorious' Unity Flats, a republican stronghold and most of the residents were not enamoured with anyone who wore a uniform or represented the 'authorities', the first policeman on scene thanked me for putting his life at risk by apprehending the alleged offender where I did, now there's gratitude. When case went to court it appeared lots of residents of Unity flats had written to the judge regarding my use of excessive force, the thief got off and I got the sack!

Another uniform down and out of work again, not for long though, through a friend I was persuaded to Join B Company, 4rd Battalion Royal Irish Rangers TA. Another uniform! I attended the regular training nights and soon became 24752164 Thompson. Serving with both the RAF Marine Craft and the Army was not unique. In 1914 a young Thomas Edward Lawrence from Tremadoc in North Wales joined the British army like many young men. In August 1922, Thomas Lawrence transferred and enlisted in the Royal Air Force as 352087 Aircraftman John Hume Ross. The reason for the change of name and service was because he had found unwanted fame during the Great War as Lawrence of Arabia and wanted to allegedly live life out of the spotlight. The media exposed him and he left the RAF in 1923. He changed his name once more to Thomas Edward Shaw and joined the Army once more, this time in the Royal Tank Corps. Desperately unhappy in the army he petitioned his former senior colleagues to allow him to return to the RAF and in particular Marine Craft Units. His wish was granted and he enlisted in the RAF again, this time as 338171 Aircraftman Thomas Edward Shaw. So I didn't set the precedence it was Lawrence of Arabia.

So off I went to Army recruit training at the home of the then Royal Irish Rangers (they were later renamed the Royal Irish Regiment) in St Patricks Barracks Ballymena and was shown our 'Lines', the Army term for accommodation. It was a ball and I finished recruit training as not only platoon leader but top recruit. One day on the parade square the drill Sergeant was barking orders at us when a three legged Jack Russell dog ran behind and him someone made a sarcastic remark. I learnt to appreciate the view of the perimeter of St Patricks Barracks, for the very same reasons I learnt the innate details of the perimeter of RAF Swinderby. During recruit training we were taught all the basic principles of being an infantry soldier, these skills would be honed when we went on exercise pretending to kill the communist hordes, a lot of whom appeared to be living in Scotland, as we seemed to fight them a lot over there. All our 'heavy' weapons training was done at a camp adjacent to HM Prison Magilligan which housed many paramilitary prisoners, I am sure those ranges were selected to either piss them off or make them jealous!! I am also positive that the music from our bar pissed also the prisoners off, though it wasn't intentional.

One day on the range we were training on the British issue General Purpose Machine Gun, better known as the 'Gimpy', this was being used as a section weapon, in the air support mode and sustained fire role. We ranged the weapons and were ready to undertake our grouping test and were given around 30 rounds to practise with, and had commenced that practise when a rabbit appeared down range, it disappeared in a puff of smoke as all 4 gunners had the same idea . . . . shoot the rabbit, I rabbit, 4 Gimpys equals no chance. If the communist hordes sent rabbits, we would win. There was always an abundance of additional days working for the TA and courses by the score, and I volunteered for almost all of them.

I quickly volunteered with a mate called Mark to undertake Radio Operator course and we were dispatched to Theiphal Barracks in

Lisburn for the first week. One day when 'walking' through the camp we were being approached by an Officer so we straightened up and began to swing our arms in a soldierly fashion. Slightly along the path was a large hole that some utility company had dug, Mark was on the inside of the path and I on the outside. We ended up squeezing together in a effort to get past the hole, this delayed progress and the officer was upon us we both mumbled '1, 2, 3' then saluted, because we were so close my right hand caught the back of his Caubeen (beret) which duly went forward over his eyes, blocked his view and he fell in the hole. Both the officer and I went into fits of laughter and I couldn't help my now muddy colleague out of the hole, other people passed us and must have wondered what the hell was going on. Once the course was finished we were promoted to Lance Corporal. The next course I undertook, following my Dads advice, was the British All Arms Static Line parachute course, there was no fucking about on that jaunt, and it was the hardest course I have ever been on in my life! But gaining the Royal Irish Rangers dark green parachute wings was overwhelming and it made my Father proud.

We were tasked to participate in a major exercise in Germany one of the objectives we were given was to protect a fictitious fuel depot from the communist hordes who would be 'played' by the Royal Marines Reserve and a squadron from 21 SAS Regiment TA. We were fucked! Through a night scope somebody noticed the odd angle of our colleague's neck; it looked like his head had been ripped backwards and his neck broken. Rumours abounded that the Marines and SAS had started playing rough and quickly someone was despatched overtly to check him out giving away the concealed position of our company HQ to all and sundry. Imagine the chaos which ensured when it was found that the guy had decided he had been on duty long enough and wanted a kip so he rotated his respirator 180 degrees so he was wearing it back to front and decided to have sit down and have a sleep, his head subsequently rolled forward. He didn't stay with us long.

During another exercise whilst on a course in the Brecon Beacons we ended up knocking down a deer with a Land Rover, the benefit of being in the TA is that there are lots of civilian skills, one of the lads on the course was a butcher from Nottingham and we had venison everything for the next two nights in the field under canvas, much better than dry ration packs and even the instructors were impressed, they had to be or they wouldn't have got any. The entrails were used to try and catch something else to eat, but it didn't work! Bad drivers yes, trappers no.

I eventually volunteered to go into Mortar platoon; through my various careers in uniform I always wanted to part of a specialist if not elite group not your run of the mill airman, soldier or sailor. The obligatory Summer camps were spent all over the place and during a camp in Thetford I qualified as a fully fledged member of the Mortar Platoon or the 'Mickey Mouse' platoon, as it was known by the rest of the Regiment. Eight months later I was promoted to Corporal.

Mortar platoon got away to the mainland for training more than any other platoon as there was no facility in Northern Ireland which allowed us to 'live fire' mortars. One of our regular haunts was Warcop in Cumbria, during one of these visits we were setting up targets on the range using a 1 tonne Landover when suddenly two rips appeared in the canvas cover of the vehicle, it was only after returning to range control we realised we had gone in the wrong direction and another unit from Northern Ireland had thought we were one of the 'moving targets' and fired on us! Thank God they were crap shots. It was worrying it looked like we would not only have to fight the communist hordes, but our own side.

The TA did and still does have a fantastic social side to it and not just at the weekends, dependant on the unit they will have their own regimental historical events that they will celebrate, for the Royal Irish Rangers, descendant from the Royal Ulster Rifles this major historical event was the Battle of the Somme, in which like many areas a generation of young men paid the ultimate sacrifice in the 'War to end all wars', after the official ceremony and the act of remembrance for the fallen there was a celebration of their sacrifice, just like the Royal Albert Hall. We also had a number of 'smokers' this usually involved lots of drink and strippers, someone cocked up after one such event for B Company and the stripper didn't get paid. Not a major issue you would think, but when the disgruntled stripper decided to ride a horse, which she incidentally kept IN her house, naked up to the camp gates accompanied by the press trying to get paid, the army were slightly pissed off. The TA in Northern Ireland was different to units on the mainland, given the security situation; we never kept weapons on the site and had to travel in convoy to another unit to pick them up every time we needed them. A lot of the time with the TA was spent on exercises and detachments outside Northern Ireland it was regular army pay and more training days than most TA would get but it wasn't the UDR which is what I had really wanted to join.

One of the most memorably secondments was to Gibraltar. The Royal Irish Rangers were to provide a 'composite' company from all 4 of the Regiments companies and go to the sunshine to train alongside the British Infantry Battalion based there. Of the approximately 120 soldiers 30 were from Northern Ireland. We drew kit from stores and packed up and departed our camp for RAF Aldergrove for our flight to RAF Brize Norton, Aldergrove was an overnight stay so in preparation for the flight early the next day we all got pissed. We left Aldergrove with no problems and arrived at RAF Brize Norton and clearly defence cuts had kicked in after I had left the RAF as we didn't even get 'transit' accommodation we camped out in a hanger in sleeping bags and ate breakfast that was cooked on a field kitchen, Christ the RAF appeared to have also done away with dining halls! After eating and washing and packing away all our gear we were processed and boarded an RAF Hercules transport aircraft, one of the RAF guys processing us recognised me from his time on the now obsolete RAF Marine Craft and advised me to sit at the rear of the 'herc'. I made sure this insider information was utilised and made sure I got a seat near the tailgate. What a fucking mistake that was, the old MCU sense of humour and practical joking had got me again, the frigging tailgate was half open I was shitting myself. To add to the indignity of my obvious fear the toilet on a Hercules is near the tailgate and guess who was sitting right next to the bastard? You've got it in one . . . . me, on a positive note I suppose I was well placed if I did actually hit myself. Let me describe the toilet on a Hercules, it is a raised stainless steel pan which has a curtain, not unlike a shower curtain, to shield you from prying eyes, oh and the RAF had also cut back on air fresheners. So here I was sitting in the back of a lumbering monster, with the back door open and a shithouse beside me, in later years it reminded me of Ryan Air. We couldn't wait to get to Gibraltar, sunshine, a couple of training exercises and lots of beer and women. We landed in blazing sunshine, off loaded our equipment and were bussed to South Barracks on the 'Rock'. As ever we were ordered to un-pack and be on parade in 10 minutes. You would think with all the organisation skills and planning that the military had you would get more than 10 minutes notice for parades! Everyone made the parade square on time and the Company Sergeant Major barked out his introduction to Gibraltar, his last comment was like a thunderbolt . . . . "All the Northern Ireland lads are to stay on camp" . . . . what? We stupidly asked why, only to be reminded we didn't ask the questions, that was his job and that it was for one simple reason "I fucking told you so". Okay we would have to drink on camp and we plotted to tell the Racial Equality Commission when we got back to the UK. The day got worse when we found out there was no bar on the camp and the nearest bar was just outside camp, which we could see but couldn't visit. One of the lads from the Royal Irish Rangers, London Company took orders and went and got us carry outs throughout the evening, it was a ridiculous situation.

Day two on the rock was the usual admin tasks for a newly arrived unit and again the Northern Irish boys were incarcerated, this was taking the piss, all the way to one of the most famous locations in the world and we were stuck on camp for no apparent reason.

The reasons became apparent the following day after the 'rock' appeared to go flaming mental with sirens. What had actually happened was that the SAS had 'neutralised' an IRA Active Service Unit as they were apparently planning to detonate a car bomb during the changing of the Honour Guard at the Governors Residence. Two males and a female from Northern Ireland had been identified, tracked and 'slotted'. Clearly the SAS did not want things confused by 30 pissed Northern Ireland lads creating havoc as they carried out their task, there could have been collateral damage. Good planning by the Army . . . eh? Let's get, what is unquestionably, the most elite military unit in the world to trace, identify, track and take out 3 Irish terrorists and just to make the event more interesting let's throw 30 Ulstermen into the equation and to make it even more interesting we will make this all happen within an area of 6.5 kilometres square! Same ethos as the DPM clothing and the Fireman's strike I suppose. The next day everyone from Northern Ireland got the whole day off to celebrate . . . . er make up for the lost time in the town. We all got plenty of beer on the back of that event and even got to take gruesome 'tourist' shots at the various locations once the local authorities had cleared up most of the mess. Just as well the IRA had stopped my leave when I was in the RAF and they had now let me get to my destination and stopped me going out, twats! But we won in the end.

The next two weeks in Gibraltar were interspaced with exercises which included FIBUA (Fighting in Built up Areas) and DIBUA (Defence in Built up Areas), training events (much to the disappointment of trees and bushes everywhere I learnt to use a chainsaw there) and the usual challenges to local sports teams. The Border with Spain was open so we also had a few nights on the piss in La Linea. We also got to do the actual touristy things such as visiting historical sites and being mugged by the Barbary Apes. One of those visits was to a place called St Michaels cave, which is in a word spectacular and we were privileged to get to see an area which is not normally open to the public. Listening to our guide describing how over thousands of years mother nature had created this beautiful site, the chemistry, physics and general science of how it came about and that fact that access was restricted as there areas that were so delicate. I always remember his aide memoire to remind me that Stalagmites originate from the ground and that Stalactites originate from the roof . . . . its simple tights come down and we all like to think we might get up something! Imagine my horror when one of these unique structures came off in my hand, thousands of years to create and one stumble by me and one of them was reduced in size by about 5 inches. I hid the artefact behind one of its now much bigger siblings and said nothing only to find out when back at camp that one guys had purposely snapped the end off one and was intending to take it back to the UK.

After a while I was asked to join another unit and duly volunteered for a position unique to the British Army in Northern Ireland, a Non Essential Regular Personnel (NERP) for the 'Northern Ireland Parcel Service', no I wasn't a postman the 'parcels' were senior & important people! I was a bit hacked off that I was now considered non essential though. I went away on a special driving course, done some further specialised training and returned to the unit, no more to be said about that chapter of my life. Sadly, my mother suddenly passed away in 1986, she was only a young woman, of 46, I took stock of my life and I decided to go 'civvy'. That plan quickly went to rats shit and I volunteered to go to another unit, went on another training course and then donned another uniform, I sought permission to document that time, but was denied by the powers that be, the opportunity to include some other hilarious tales had gone, sorry folks a silent chapter. After 4 years in that uniform and following what I will call a careers advice visit from some local personalities that uniform also went in the wardrobe, it was only because of their respect for my father that I wasn't buried in it, I was just a little bit bruised and battered. So what the hell was I to do now? I spoke to a former colleague who had some contacts, my Dad called in some favours from his Royal Ulster Constabulary and former Army colleagues and my next adventure was about to begin. 24752164 Thompson had left the army building.

CHAPTER 10

ħෆS Raleigh and beyond

Ha ha Lawrence of Arabia hadn't been in the Royal Navy!! But he was in the RAF twice, so that's a draw. I left Northern Ireland in January 1990, flew to Heathrow and boarded a train for Plymouth . . . . déjà vu or what? I was joined by a few others soon to be Royal Navy recruits from Northern Ireland; one in particular stands out a tall ginger haired lad called Brian. We had far too much beer on the train and the other passengers complained about our swearing. We arrived at Plymouth station and boarded a bus, to HMS Raleigh, it reminded me of 1977 and joining the RAF, only this time the bus from the train station turned right instead of left. We arrived at HMS Raleigh to find that unlike the RAF the Royal Navy had retained 'transit' accommodation or as they called them messes. Next Day I took another oath, was issued another uniform and D230948M Thompson had entered another building. I was again going to be trained to fight the communist hordes, this time Royal Navy style. This should be fun the Royal Navy apparently trained James Bond didn't they, would this eventually mean birds, gadgets and fast cars???

I was assigned to a class with both male and female members. The first week in the Royal Navy was all too familiar to me, with more bloody inoculations, kit issue, haircuts & inspections etc. and the Training

62

personnel quoting what appeared to be every 30 seconds "the RN has a strict no touch policy, this is to ensure that male and female recruits do not walk round holding hands or cuddling and kissing". I knew from my previous experiences that homosexuality was strictly frowned upon in the RAF and Army; at first it appears that the Navy was frowning upon heterosexuality! Thank God I had got the wrong end of the stick, males holding hands etc. was deemed to be just as bad. I always remember being told the following by my Grandfather:

"When I was a boy, being homosexual was Illegal",

"Then they reduced the age to 21",

"Then 18"

"Then 'they' had their own bars"

"Trust me son, by the time you're my age it'll be compulsory".

I've heard them same comments scores of times but this was the first time I had heard this, not for a minute do I believe my Grandfather was the author, but he clearly thought it was one of his outlooks on life that I would benefit from if he shared it! During that first week I was more like a street pastor to many of the younger recruits who were in the same position I had been in 23 years previously when joining RAF. Some left but most didn't. As the oldest (30 years of age) I wasn't always treated by the training staff as a recruit, we would have conversations without shouting! I became a little complacent I made the fatal mistake one morning of winking at a Chief Wren, upon answering a question, after which she whispered in my ear:

'Don't do that again, trust me, I can fuck you in more than one way' . . . . message understood.

She was the same size as my RAF recruiting Sergeant, I believed her. Due to my age and that fact that I appeared to have a migrant attraction to the Armed Forces I was quickly made class leader. There is a clear distinction between the Royal Navy uniform and that of the other two branches of the armed forces and when the great British public see sailors wearing their 'white fronts' what they don't realise is when they are issued they are more or less yellow. There must be some executive with Unilever who is rubbing his hands at that. Unilever by the way, make washing powder! We spent so much of our time washing, time after time, bloody white fronts. They were more or less boiled to within an inch of their lives in industrial washing machines which had queues beside them every night. The Navy should have employed Dot Cotton from the TV soap Eastenders; she would have made Mr Papadopoulos a millionaire washing white fronts!

For me Royal Navy recruit training was pretty easy, I'd done it all before and knew what to expect, the hardest thing was learning to do drill differently. All three branches of the armed forces salute but they all salute differently, Army—longest way up, longest way down, RAF—longest way up, shortest way down, Royal Navy—shortest way up, and shortest way down. The Royal Navy are immensely proud of the fact that they are the Senior Service and rightly so, they ensure that recruits are aware of that history and its impact on today's Navy. Small things like explaining why the uniform is as it is, did you know Royal Navy officers sit down to toast the Queen, why? Simple really, in older times the space between decks was low so there was little room to stand and the monarch of the day accepted this protocol. There are many everyday sayings and events that originate from the Royal Navy of old, that's one thing, recruit training taught me. Allegedly the origins of the Twenty One gun salute come from the RN. In the past ships would discharge their guns before entering harbours to so show their potential hosts that they were friendly, they would not have had time to re-load before coming within range of the shore batteries.

Why 21, this was rumoured to be due to the limited storage space of the precious 'Black powder', they couldn't waste any more. The Royal Navy treats shore bases as ships, 'stone frigates' as they are sometimes known. I remember going to HMS Cambridge from RAF Mountbatten for a dentist appointment and whilst walking over some grass a Royal Navy Petty Officer threw a lifebelt at me and a colleague. At the time I thought it was because we had beaten them at football, it was only afterwards that I realised the grass was symbolic of the sea! So he wasn't pissed off and trying to injure me he was trying to help, I never did get the chance to thank him, but I'm a strong walker and got myself out of difficulties as did my colleague, must have been due to that training with the QCS! HMS Raleigh was 'dry' for all recruits, in other words there was no NAAFI bar, just as well because most of my class were not old enough to buy a drink. Back to being a recruit, we moved after the first week into our more permanent 'billets'.

As ever there was drill and believe me we needed it, it appeared that RN selection had a caveat that you could get in if you couldn't swing your arms alternatively to your legs, the military term for this is 'tick tocking' and we had more 'tick tockers' than a Swiss clock factory. For the instructor this was going to be a challenge. More weapons training, this was interesting because I could strip and re-assemble the SA80, the now standard firearm of the British military, as quick as the instructor and he would get openly pissed off. Again we were given enough inoculations to last a lifetime; if I ad fallen overboard at that stage I would have probably sunk I had that many holes in me. The ever present physical training to get us fit to fight, tire us out and test our stamina. We had one particular PE instructor that would constantly refer to me as 'Paddy' given my background I thought that was a name you should give to someone from the Irish Republic and found it slightly uneasy being called that, so I told him . . . . 'give me 10'. Why oh why is that the standard response from every PT instructor that has ever existed? Do they teach them that phrase during training? I've got reasonably broad shoulders and it's not from doing lots of scheduled training, I'm sure it's down to doing 3 recruit courses and doing so many bloody press ups. Like all recruit training you train hard to fight easy and the main task is to get through training without getting injured and discharged or 'back classed' i.e. joining a class behind yours because you can't grasp things. The trick is to eat as much as you can and sleep when you can, as all recruit training is designed to test your limits of stamina, hunger and general tiredness. As HMS Raleigh was also the Royal Navy catering school the food was of varying quality, not bad but not consistently good. The in joke of the day was that the Royal Navy catering course was the hardest course in the Navy, as no bugger had passed it!!! Despite my earlier reference to remaining friends with the cooks & store men, military cooks were still the subject of 'banter. Most servicemen will know the joke about "Ok who called the cook a cunt"? only to have some wag retort "What I want to know is who called the cunt a cook", they do their best with very strict potion control and in the field military cooks and chefs perform wonders, even with dry 24 hour ration packs, if you're hungry you'll eat it believe me. A few weeks into recruit training we were taken for a visit around a warship. During the visit to the ships the ships cooks provided us with what are known as 'Bag meals' this is a brown paper bag with some sandwiches, a piece of fruit, a bag of crisps and a yoghurt and a carton of drink. The sandwiches are inevitably ham or cheese, the fruit is an apple, orange or banana, the crisps will be ready salted, the yoghurt is always bloody strawberry and the carton is always orange juice. It contains all the stuff you wouldn't choose for a packed lunch, on a positive note there were no crunchy peanut butter sandwiches., as soon as we got back to HMS Raleigh I found myself putting my hand up when they asked for those wishing to volunteer for service on Submarines, I remember getting seasick in the RAF and the nice Petty Officer said you got extra pay! The chef's better be good on submarines I thought.

The most enjoyable part of RN recruit training has to be the damage control and fire fighting training. You're basically placed in burning containers and shown how to put the fires out and placed in front of a domestic cooker with burning oil on it, this is tipped over and hurtles towards you in a fireball, it hits a wall of water, makes you shit yourself and disperses. For damage control you are placed in a tank that is full of pipes and holds and you have to stop the ingress of water before either the tank overflows or you drown, simple! I wasn't too fazed by either as I had done this exact training at the same site when undergoing my RAF Motor Boat Crew training. I was a bit disappointed that in nearly 10 years since I had first undertaken a fire fighting and damage control course that the RN hadn't fixed any of the holes and had not made the efforts to stop the containers catching fire defence cuts I suppose. After a period of time at HMS Raleigh you are unleashed on the public . . . i.e. you can go off camp. First destination for most Royal Navy recruits is a pub called the Carbeile Inn, in Torpoint which basically served lots of alcohol and served food of gargantuan proportions. I would say there are very few, if any, RN personnel who have come through HMS Raleigh that have not visited the Carbeile, even if they didn't drink. Those welcome runs ashore still had a curfew attached to them and there was more than one recruit who found himself/herself in the shit for being 'adrift', that's RN speak for being late. HMS Raleigh initial training passed without incident and I was lucky enough to lead the Honour Guard as my class, once more, ended up as the champion class. Even though I had experienced this before it was still an achievement, and I was chuffed to bits. After the passing out parade those of us who were going into seaman's branch trades moved our kit across a forecourt and unpacked in our new billets. We didn't go straight into Part 2 training we were selected to represent the Royal Navy in a BOVRAL games, this was basically military Olympics between the chosen RN, and Army recruits. The competition was to be held at the Army Armoured Corps Training centre in Bovington. We kicked arse and won everything the

Army recruits were 'giving 10' like there was no tomorrow and were mostly pissed off with losing out on the firing range. I scored 98% in the final shoot out with the Army instructors, they accused the RN of cheating saying that a new recruit couldn't learn to shoot like that in 6 weeks and they were right, that 4 year undisclosed period had taught me how to use a 9mm Browning pistol very efficiently. In the swimming events we had an advantage a recruit from St Lucia and I swear fish couldn't have caught him in the water, he was like a bloody torpedo, and he was finishing races before others had finished one length. He was lucky with his talent he would be able to swim away from the communist hordes.

We were given a tour of the Royal Armoured Corps Tank museum and to my shock there was a former member of my Dads 'A Team' working there and he recognised me, small world. We had an overnight stay challenging the army at drinking games, which ended in a draw, and left for HMS Raleigh the next day, after nicking some souvenirs in the form of plaques. We had the weekend to visit the Carbeile and try to get laid before commencing Seamanship training.

On the Monday we were issued a white lanyard and an engraved clasp knife all of which we would wear to denote we were now on Part 2 Training—Seamanship. Clearly we were supposed to either hang ourselves or slit our wrists when the we couldn't swim or march any further away from the communist hordes. First benefit of Part 2 training is that you can go out every night, a luxury that wasn't over looked and the Carbeile profits went up! Seamanship training was geared more to those recruits who were going to become RN General Service personnel or 'Skimmers' as submariners knew them. We would practise Replenishment At Sea signals, certain 'pipes' using the bosuns call, bends and hitches and tying up fictitious ships. As with all training regime the further you progress the less rigid it became, but it wasn't relaxed so to speak, we still had inspections etc. and by now we could out swim, out run and out polish the communist hordes, oh and help them put out fires and plug holes, to boot. After 3 weeks of Seamanship training we had our 'drafts' (postings) confirmed and I along with 5 others had been selected for 'boats', better known as HM Submarines. We set off for HMS Dolphin in Gosport.

CHAPTER 11

HMS Dolphin and beyond

We arrived at HMS Dolphin and were shown to our mess, not a transit mess a proper mess, ye ha! The Guard on the gate told us to go to Nelsons and Emmas, the submariners adopted pub in Gosport. Every garrison town has pubs that are adopted by units, at RAF Mountbatten it was the New Inn in Turnchapel, HMS Raleigh was the Carbiele, in Torpoint and it appeared that Gosport was no different. The main benefit of HMS Dolphins location was that it was right next door to the Royal Naval Hospital at Haslar . . . . NURSES! Dad always told me there were only two certs in life, taxes and student nurses. I also held strong the personal belief that beauty was only a light switch away as long as it had a pulse. Not very diverse, sexist yes, but I was young and daft. We unpacked, had our 'scran' which was of an excellent standard and headed off to Nelsons and Emmas, and were we spent nearly the whole weekend and most of our money.

We reported to the Submarine training school at 08:55 sharp on the Monday morning and the first thing that struck me was a huge picture of a Submarine and another of a ship with crosshairs on it with the words "there are only two types of ships, Submarines and Targets" . . . I'm going to like these guys I thought. The other noticeable sign were the letters F.O.H.S.B emblazoned on the wall, I would find out the two meanings of this abbreviation later in my career. As ever, as the oldest and with previous service I was again made class leader. First task was our 'tour' of the Submarine training school to get orientated then off to stores to get rid of our 'skimmers' kit and get 'proper uniform' issued. Submariners wear fire retardant uniform. Initial submarine training was in two parts, basic submariner training then trade specific training. The first three weeks was a mixture of technical classroom training and practical training on board a decommissioned 'O' Class submarine HMS Oberon. During this phase we had further medicals and were put in a hyperbaric chamber and taken down to certain depths to make sure our ear drums didn't burst and that our heads didn't explode! We were also to undertake submarine escape training; this would take place in the Submarine Escape Training Tank (SETT). This was a fresh-water filled tank that dominated the Gosport skyline and can be seen for miles it was just over 10 storeys high, with the actual tank being 30 metres deep. Looking from the top of the tank the water is crystal clear all the way to the bottom; you can see two hatches at the base and a number of 'havens' on the sides. All submariners must do this training or you're out. You do a 'dry' escape and a 'wet' escape and they are totally different with the exception that you hopefully go up. For the 'Dry' escape you don a special submarine escape suit which is waterproof, has a hood and a built in lifejacket. You then enter an 'escape pod' and close the lower hatch your escape suit is then plugged into an air supply which inflates the lifejacket, here's the scary bit that is all the air supply you get, in the meantime the 'escape pod' is filling with water. Once the escape pod is filled the pressure with the exterior of the hatch is neutralised so the upper hatch can be opened and you begin to float out. Surprisingly there is a nice Royal Navy diver there to meet you and hold you at the base of the tank before releasing you, but after you give him thumbs up. You start off slowly and pick up momentum on the way to the surface and hit it like a bloody Polaris missile. I had visions of me shooting out over the top of the rim and falling nearly 30 metres to my death . . . . fastest way up, fastest way down, that's a new one!

The secret is the lifejacket, as it is inflated under pressure the reduction in water pressure as you shoot towards the surface allows the air in the lifejacket to expand and this provides you with the much needed air. The 'wet' escape is a different kettle of fish. You enter one of the 'havens' near the base of the tank it starts to fill more or less to shoulder height, you take a deep breath swim out of it and breathe out all the way to the surface, if not your lungs explode! You feel on a number of occasions that you're going to run out of air but the thought of your lungs exiting your chest keeps you going. It's a fantastic experience but not one I'd want to do for real. Submarine rescue is particularly difficult as the world seen with the Russian submarine Kursk. All the instructors are part of the RNs Submarine Parachute Assistance Group (SPAG). These guys fly out to the middle of the ocean, parachute out and assist in the rescue of submariners. That's the theory, but the depth will limit their ability to help after 30 meters it's by Deep Submersible Rescue Vessel (DSRV) and there are very few of them.

In addition to all this exciting stuff there were written exams and a week away in the Welsh mountains on 'adventure training' for that I ended up as the bloody cook. Now if the RAF Marine craft nutters were the WOPs and the Marine fitters then the whole of a submarine crew fitted that bill for the RN, submariners are crazy, in the nicest sense, maybe they have to be, as practical jokers they are world class. One of our instructors told us of an occasion when he and his first wife had been to a wedding and returned home smashed, during the night he accidentally went to the toilet in bed, not uncommon with drunks, it was different this time though he didn't piss himself! In an effort to cover up his misdemeanour he carefully positioned his 'parcel' between the buttocks of his sleeping wife and then woke her up, she was as to be expected mortified. For months she couldn't console herself and was talking about seeking 'treatment' for her affliction, he told her the truth and eventually they divorced and she was enshrined in his memory as his 'first wife'.

Towards the end of our submarine part one training we were taken aboard HMS Oberon and shown how dangerous a fire was on board a submarine, they didn't set fire to it the instructors set off a smoke grenade which quickly spread throughout the boat. Now 'O' boats were not ergonomically designed so once you're in blackout conditions you start banging your head of every piece of equipment that is sticking out, I was black and blue by the time the smoke cleared one of my colleagues who was around 6 feet tall was heard to be constantly whimpering after numerous sickening thuds. Again it was a great experience but we wouldn't want to have done it for real. Following part one training we were split into separate groups who would undertake part two training as either Tactical Systems Operators (TS) or Sonar Operators (SO). Submarines don't have windows so they listen, the Sonar Operators found the targets, Tactical Systems Operators collated the information from all the varied sensors and tried to establish a firing solution on targets. It is noise that gives a submarines position away, and noise travels underwater hence the name the Silent Service. These trades no longer exist in the RN; the service has evolved them into having Operator Maintainers. Submariners are cautious regarding speaking about the operational aspect of the service and protective of the service as a whole, so I won't go into specific detail on the above roles. There was a standing joke that if you wanted to know what was happening in the submarine service all you had to do was ask a taxi driver in Helensbugh, but that was a rumour started by skimmers. If it hadn't been, all the taxis in Helensburgh would have been driven by the communist hordes.

One of the most poignant events I have ever seen was the gathering of the Submarine Old Comrades Association or SOCA as it is known. This is a mix of world war two veterans and more recent ex servicemen, when they read out the role of Honour for those submariners lost during that conflict, these fellow submariners wept openly for those who had passed, the stories they told were amazing. I had the privilege of accompanying a South African veteran around the Royal Navy Submarine Museum we spent hours going around it and he was able to tell me much more about some of the artefacts than was written on the museum narratives. Oh and he still didn't like the Germans or the Japanese, he lost two older brothers in the war.

Upon the completion of Submarine part two training we were drafted to specific 'boats' mine was based in Plymouth and was the newest in her class, HMS Triumph. The rest of the class were allocated other Trafalgar class boats based in Plymouth or 'Bombers' based at Faslane, in Scotland.

CHAPTER 12

HMNB Faslane & beyond

I made my way to Plymouth by train, came out of the station and turned right again, this time en route to HMS Drake. Another bloody transit mess, the skimmers were taking the piss me thinks. Their joke only lasted until Monday when I was allocated a billet in the Submariners accommodation block. I reported to the Submarine Squadron office and was then sent to join the Ops team training facility, what?

I thought I was joining a submarine, but apparently HMS Triumph had left for Scotland without me. The footprint of HMS Drake was huge in comparison to HMS Dolphin and had the usual rigid skimmer regime, it adjoined the Royal Navy Dockyard in Plymouth so getting lost was easy and you could waste hours just going to stores to pick something up or getting something signed.

I was still not a submariner, I had not undergone part three training to gain my 'Dolphins' the world wide recognised symbol of a fully qualified submariner, so here I am not accepted by the skimmers because my submariners fire retardant working dress identified me as a non skimmer and not fully accepted by the submariners as I was devoid of dolphins. The tactical trainer allowed me to continue developing my TS skills which would hopefully help when I eventually joined my boat.

Within a week I had met other members of my boats crew and was informed that we would meet the boat in HM Naval Base Faslane, Scotland. Practical joking wasn't restricted to the RAF Marine Craft my new 'oppos' told me to take all my kit to Scotland so I packed it all up joined them in a hire car and we set off for Scotland. We took it in turns to drive and arrived at Faslane in the late evening, my oppos quickly dumped their kit on their 'sea racks' and headed off to Helensburgh for a drink. I was shown to the 'bomb shop' or torpedo compartment given a temporary bunk and told to do something with all the crap that I had brought along. It took me three trips to the dockside to collect all my kit and I had to distribute it throughout the boat as the locker space, OBVIOUSLY, was limited.

The boat was palatial compared to the single decked Oberon class boat and surprisingly big. I eventually got packed away and one of the crew offered to share a taxi with me to the adopted pub in Helensburgh, the Imperial Hotel, or the Imps as it was known. We arrived in the Imps and I was introduced to other members of the crew who were clearly afraid that prohibition was coming and were trying to consume as much alcohol as they could before last orders, I joined in. Shortly afterwards a few drunk guys came into the bar and the mood changed, I went to the toilet and was joined by the two very drunk blokes who were clearly planning to 'start on' the submariners, time to think. One went into a cubicle and the other struggled to keep upright whilst urinating I bounced his head off the toilet wall and he was out like a light, I never thought that would happen, no noise, no scuffle, nothing. One of my crewmates came into the toilets and saw the fella on the floor and commented that people shouldn't get so drunk they pass out. As that comment was made the second drunk exited the cubicle and stooped to see what was wrong with his mate mumbling something about "fucking submariners" and that "there was only one type of marine and that was a Royal Marine" with that comment my new crew mate laid him out, it wasn't hard they were both paralytic and out of it. The crewmate took £10 for our troubles and bought me a beer at the bar. After a while to drunks emerged from the toilets exited and clearly went home, none the wiser to what had happened. In an effort to get himself out of the shit my crewmate told the rest of me new crew that it was all me!

I launched into me part three training with a vengeance, there was no way I wanted to be a 'part three' for too long. The reason? As a part three you are not allowed 'down time' no resting in the mess and when off watch you're expected to get tasks signed off, not lounge about. The working routine at sea was six hours on, six hours off, but when alongside it was 08:00 until 16:00 as a part three you were expected to work later than 16:00 and rightly so. Part three training teaches you about a submarines vital systems and you have to know how and where to isolate all the systems on board, you get tested by the crew and when you've finally got your part three task book signed off you take an oral test, if you pass you're recommended to the Captain to receive your Dolphins. I would get plenty of time to learn the systems as my boat was in Faslane to undertake maintenance and then 'work-up', an intense testing of the crew and the boat. One of the very first jobs I was tasked to do was to help strip the protective housing surrounding the nuclear reactor! That was fun!

Work-up is done alongside and at sea, one of the scenarios was that the crew had to deal with a riot on the dockside and suitable volunteers had been sought from the rest of HMNB Faslane to play the role of the rioters, most of them were skimmers or medically downgraded submariners. There was another ex-army crew member and I that had both received riot training for Northern Ireland and we asked if we could 'arrest' the ringleaders, snatch squad style, that wish was granted.

We sneaked up to the side of the rioters and then flew out grabbing the poor sod that had been told to act as ringleader; he crapped himself, took a swing at us and was promptly pole axed by a head butt with a steel helmet, ouch. Bloody whistles and shouting went on all over the place the exercise was stopped and we were accused of being too rough, this was a bloody riot, I don't do diplomacy and skimmers can't do riots I thought. We also undertook some force protection and site security exercises, which incidentally included the two bruised Royal Marines from the Imps!

I had been part of the crew for just over a week and hadn't been to sea yet, let alone having been on a submarine that dived. Remembering that the death of a submarine and her crew normally starts with noise I learnt all the sarcastic remarks such as "this is a submarine, not a fucking tambourine", easy way to stop them is to be quite. The day finally came when we were to commence the at sea element of work-up. The boat was stored with provisions and the Flag Officer Sea Training Team (FOST) joined us, these were the guys that would test the crew and the boat to their limits. My first real dive was apprehensively exciting, waiting to hear all compartments to report dry was a bonus! I quickly learnt that submariners do not close hatches they shut them, they close doors. Hatches are watertight, doors aren't. We quickly slipped into our at sea routine and I was also going to be able to do TS work, as I had been trained to do.

The guys in the TS department on board the boat were absolutely brilliant at their job, I was going to have good teachers (Thanks, Lee, Dutchy and Buster) and a high standard to achieve to be part of this fraternity. We left Faslane and transited down the River Clyde towards our exercise area within minutes the boat was on fire, of course it was an exercise by the FOST team, the BA attack teams on submarines wear red tabards and when they are heading towards a fire be it real or for exercise you had better get out of their way. They don't take prisoners, if they can't go round you they will either go over you or through you. The internal hatches are all shut and the smoke contained, until the attack team can assess the gravity of the fire, whilst they're doing this there is another fire crew suiting up to tackle the fire if needed and the whole crew don Built in Breathing System (BIBS) masks. The exercise fire was quickly extinguished and we were ordered to dive. On your first full dive you probably notice more creaks and noises than you ever will, it is fascinating an eventual downward angle at slow speed, they only way you can tell your going down is by looking at the depth counter, not always a good idea. I was learning to speak 'submariner', as they have their own jargon like most groups of individuals and they speak in abbreviations such as UWT, SNAPs, SMP the list is endless. The FOST team must have thought I had potential as an actor as whenever they needed someone to be 'made up' as if injured it always seemed to be me they picked on, I had bloody nails sticking out of my head, a bolt in my eye, burns, cuts bruises the whole lot was applied by a very competent 'make up' artist, Halloween parties would have been fun in his house. My new crew must have thought I was very unlucky. There were numerous exercises and because torpedoes are expensive, and bloody dangerous, we fired 'water shots' at fishing boats. This was effectively done by filling a torpedo tube with water and forcing it out of the tube, I was now at sea on an £160,000,000 water pistol.

We also had to undertake an 'evolution' which involved coming alongside the US Navy Submarine Support Ship the USS Simon Lake, this was her last exercise with a submarine as she was due to decommission, that's the wrong thing to tell a British Submariner, we got invited on board and upon leaving helped ourselves to souvenirs such as the ships brass plaques and various items of US Naval clothing. The whole week was similar to recruit training, sleep deprivation, unusual occurrences, fire and famine, but we came through with a good pass and were deemed operational. It helped me get to grips with all the submarine systems as the FOST team made everything leak! We transited back to Faslane, passing that landmark at Inverkip that is known to all submariners as the FBC or the Fucking Big Chimney of the power station and disembarked the FOST team. Despite the popular belief, you're not constantly in the dark on a submarine, it's 'white lighting' all the way, apart from night time when its either 'Red lighting' (when on the surface) or 'Black Lighting' (when using the periscope) in the control room.

In peacetime Submarines generally travel on the surface and there is one slight problem with that, they are built to go underwater and roll worse that the RAF LRRSC. Submarines are pigs on the surface in rough weather and it is not possible to get anyone on the casing, underwater they are fine it's like being on an airplane they effectively 'fly' underwater. So in rough weather the boat can smell of puke. It is even worse when the boat discharges its slop, drain and sewage tank that vents inboard as well and there is a brief smell of shit, not what you want on a big black tube. That is why deodorant and aftershave is frowned upon, it puts the boats atmosphere 'out of spec' and is hard to get rid of, I remember a bottle of perfume, a present for a loved one, was somehow broken smashed in the forward crew bunk space and the place smelt like a brothel for what seemed forever.

My wish had also been granted with regards to the chefs (they were never referred to as cooks by the crew, remember the hardest course in the RN?), they were great what they achieved in such a small galley was pure magic. Fresh bread baked every day, steaks on Saturday night, patrol breakfasts (this was a full English with mushrooms) the day before you got into port, Grapefruit segments on a Sunday morning, it did get predictable but none the less the standard was superb at least it was on HMS Triumph. As boats make their own fresh water the only thing that limits endurance is the capacity to feed the crew. We spent our last night in the Imps and the Akash Indian Restaurant taking the piss out of the proprietor, Dennis and eating lime pickle for bets!

The next day we departed HMNB Faslane, transited the River Clyde and the Firth of Clyde and set sail for Plymouth our home base, three days into the sailing I had passed my Part three training and was awarded my 'dolphins' in the traditional manner i.e. taking a glass of rum and catching the dolphins in my teeth. I'd done it and was enthused with the knowledge that once we got back to Plymouth one of the crew was leaving and I was to get a proper 'sea rack' out with the bomb shop. The only damper on my celebrations was that the Soviet Union had announced to the world it was breaking up. I had spent my adult life in uniform training to stifle the advances of the communist hordes and now some of them had given up. This would certainly reduce the bruises on my forehead, the bomb shop racks are either clamped on top of or underneath the weaponry carried so the space is even smaller than the actual sea racks and they themselves are barely bigger than a coffin, and in fact some guys had to get out of their racks to turn over. Another myth regarding modern submarines is 'hot bunking' i.e. sharing a sea rack, it is not unheard of but it is very rare on modern boats. The trip back to Plymouth was generally uneventful and I quickly slipped into the on board routine. We arrived back and had 4-5 days off, before slotting back into our alongside routine, this was normally undertaking training, playing sports or getting the boat ready for its next patrol. In the meantime Yugoslavia had decided they didn't want to be part of the communist hordes anymore and they gave up also. It was beginning to look like we would soon have no one to fight with. But we had heard that George W Bush and his puppy Tony Blair were concocting a cunning plan to find a new enemy.

Dad 'washing' in the desert

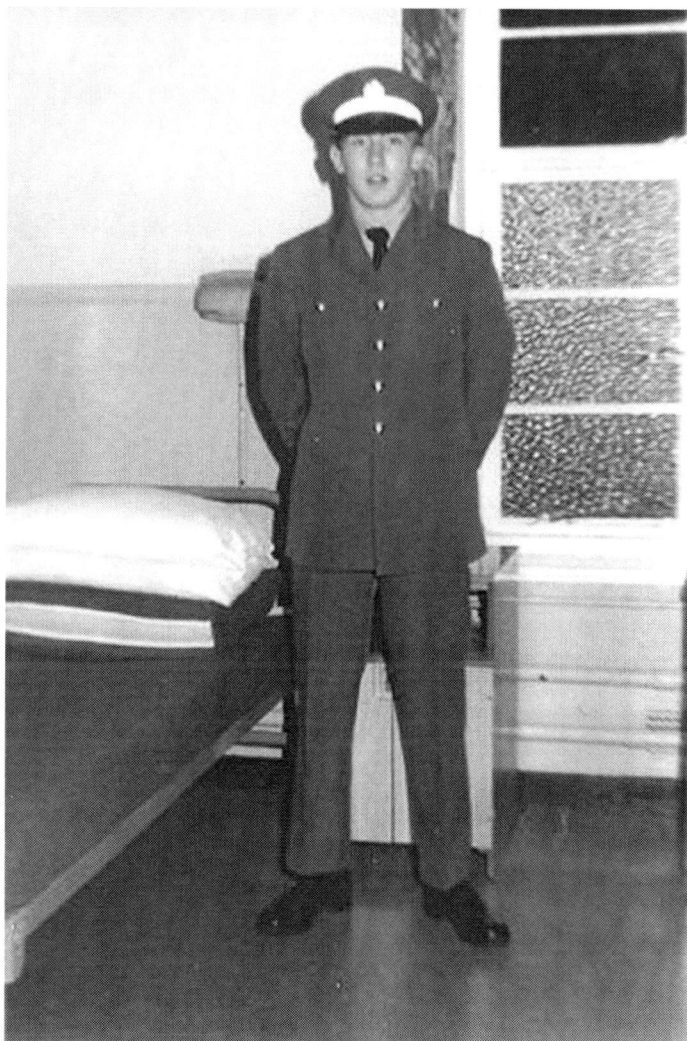

J8136665 Aircraftman Thompson

RTTL Mk2 2757 at speed

Pinnace 1388 at her moorings off Tenby

HM Submarine Triumph

24752164 Ranger Thompson (face uncovered)

D230948M Thompson, third from the right on the front row

Saying Goodbye to Diego Garcia

The author with Krakatau in the background.

New Entry 83 (author, back row, forth from the right)

CHAPTER 13

We're all buddies on boats

After a few weeks got our patrol orders, although we, the crew, were deemed operational the boat would need to be tested for acoustics and noise shorts, in other words the RN has to be sure we were quite, this is tested at a once secret but now well known facility off the West Coast of Scotland called BUTEC (British Underwater Test and Evaluation Centre). The range consists of a noise range to the East of the Isle of South Rona, and another range for torpedo testing between the Isle of Raasay and Applecross on the mainland. The noise range is approximately one mile long and divided into a series of 26 blocks within which there are a large array of acoustic sensors. We would do a number of test runs and if we were quiet enough we'd be off to the Atlantic Undersea Test and Evaluation Centre (AUTEC) which belonged to the US Navy and was on Andros Island, the benefit of that . . . . it's the largest of the 26 inhabited Bahamian Islands, yes the Bahamas. Skimmer training staff told me I'd only see the world though a periscope.

Following AUTEC we were to participate in a major NATO exercise off the East coast of the US and then have 10 days R&R in Fort Lauderdale, now this was the Navy I'd heard of. We still acted on a war footing every time we went to sea, because there was a constant game with the communist hordes, we would try and sneak up on them and they would try and sneak up on us. We passed BUTEC with flying colours, participated in another exercise off the West coast of Scotland and then headed for the Bahamas. We arrived off Andros Island in the Bahamas after a reasonably uneventful crossing of the Atlantic. The only real incident was during an exercise on board someone was closing one of the watertight doors on board and trapped the thumb of a junior engineering officer, he squealed with pain the door was opened and a rather inflamed thumb was bandaged, his pain was subdued with paracetamol but his embarrassment couldn't be tamed. Especially as crew members would put both thumbs in the air and sing 'fan daby dozy', like the children's TV characters the Crankies, every time he passed them, he was really pissed off by the time we arrived. We would play bingo on board to relieve the boredom, the only drawback was a single number was called everyday at 1pm; this could potentially take us 90 days to play.

We went through a similar series of exercises as we had at BUTEC and the yanks couldn't find us either, result! The communist hordes would have to listen very carefully to find us! One frightening thing did happen and that was by way of us being hit by an inert practise torpedo launched from a British helicopter, it bounced off the rear end of the boat but thankfully didn't cause any damage. Then we were allowed ashore on Andros Island roughly every other day, but only for short periods at a time. We did however get to swim in a Blue hole which is an inland sinkhole in the middle of the jungle, the experience was weird half the fish and crabs in the bloody thing looked prehistoric, it was like something out of Journey to the Centre of the Earth or Land of the Dinosaurs but in miniature. We got to eat in the US Navy restaurant which was another experience, Ice cream and sodas by the bucketful and steaks the size of which we had only seen on TV or in the movies. AUTEC passed it was time to kick ass, Triumph style. Once more we embarked stores, but this time we also embarked a British Army Major from the Devon and Dorset Regiment, he was to be our guest.

We stowed the boat for sea and set off for our exercise starting point, we had complete faith in our Captain he was superb and respected not only within the Royal Navy, but by other partners within NATO, he was tactically astute and his man management skills were second to none, he eventually became the Queens Harbour Master HMNB Faslane. His crew were as loyal as could be and he had a wickedly dry sense of humour. Our first series of runs were against a French ship and we were able to take underwater photographs of her propellers and hull undetected, bragging rights with the French sorted. We then had to engage the USS Baton Rouge a US Los Angeles-class submarine. We quickly found her and slotted in to her 'Stern arcs' for non submariners that is the blind spot at the back of a submarine. We followed her until the Captain decided the time was right and then we blasted out "Danger Zone" by Kenny Loggins to let them know if we had been the communist hordes they would have been dead! We then buggered off and 'sank' a US Trocadero class destroyer, before starting on the Baton Rouge again, once more we found her and tracked her and this time we shot her with "Take my breath away" by Berlin. The Captain was obviously a Top Gun fan. The Baton Rouge clearly didn't learn much, in February 1992, she allegedly collided with a Russian Sierra-class boat, one of the newest and quietest boats belonging to the communist hordes. Baton Rouge was tracking the Sierra off Murmansk when they lost contact with the target who then struck her from below. It was clearly embarrassing for both nations but from a submariners point of view nobody was hurt. What submariners do is probably as near to war as you can get without killing anyone, but it's close to the edge and as a world community no one wants to see other submariners die during peacetime.

We finished the exercise and headed into Fort Lauderdale. As soon as we were alongside and secured we were allocated our hotels and given our subsistence. Submariners stay in hotels when in ports which have no military accommodation nearby and get subsistence to provide meals. Skimmers stay on board and get those bloody brown bag meals. Submariners also get extra money in the form of submarine pay. Those who were unfortunate enough to pick up the duty were left behind. Remember F.O.H.S.B at the Submarine Training School? It means "Fall Out Harbour Stations Below" in other words you're on shore leave until told to return. We arrived at the hotel and most of us threw our bags in our rooms, headed for the bar and the pool to make plans for the evening. The destination was a place called Bobby Rubinos, which had fed British submariners for years, newbie's had to try the world famous Ribs and Onion loaf. We then headed for the beachfront bars and ended up in a bar called Hooters, I'll leave you to imagine the bar staff, if I described them you wouldn't believe me, but they do have a website, go see for yourself. Hooters was also the haunt of American sailors for the very same reason the Brits went there.

Our runs ashore were in civvies the US Sailors had to go ashore in uniform . . . unlucky. We told the manager who we were and what we doing in the US, just in case he knew a taxi driver in Helensburgh and we took great pleasure in telling him had kicked the arse of the USS Baton Rouge, he was impressed and gave us beer. We got extremely drunk and promised to return. We did return to Hooters on a regular basis and on one occasion the crew of the USS Baton Rouge turned up, 'Tank' the manager and our new best friends told them he didn't like losers and kicked them out after a bit of a plea from the crew of Triumph he let them back in, if we were going to take the piss out of them we needed them in the same bar! As ever stupid games ensued we played them at Navy draughts or checkers as the yanks would call it, instead of counters we used white and dark rum! Another challenged was to see who could eat the most Buffalo wings, these were excruciatingly hot and spicy wings and we lost that one, the yanks rolled out a beast that ate them like crisps while most of us Brits were out front being sick after three at the most. Is it any wonder that buffalos are nearly extinct their wings are tiny, it's pretty obvious that such tiny wings couldn't hold up a half ton woolly cow, they were clearly stupid animals, not only that, like frogs legs, they taste like chicken.

One of the things that happens to all Royal Naval personnel overseas is that ex-pats in one form or another will be try to be friendly to sailors, in particular if there are sailors from their own home town or even county. We used to call it *"Dial a Sailor"*, Fort Lauderdale was no different. Because I was from Northern Ireland I ended up being paired to a guy called 'Rick', again submariner practical joking kicked in. Rick O'Connor visited HMS Triumph and I was his designated host I could hardly understand his thick Irish brogue but I muddled through. At the end of the visit he invited to his home to have dinner with his family, I couldn't refuse. On the way to his house we stopped at a sports bar and had far too many beers, Rick was driving. We left the sports bar to arrive at a very smart suburban house which had two flagpoles outside one flying the Stars and Stripes the other sporting the Irish tricolour, for me things became a little uncomfortable. We exited his car and his family were lined up like the Von Trapps from the Sound of Music and he introduced them one by one, every one of them spoke with an Irish brogue. We sat down to a lovely home cooked meal and during the conversation I asked when Rick and his family had left Ireland to move to the US. His answer was "we've never been there"; "you've never been to Ireland? Any of you" I asked "no" was his reply. Intrigued, I asked how come he had such a strong brogue and how all his family spoke with an Irish accent, his answer had me gobsmacked. "We've taken elocution lessons" he said. Ricks wife drove me back to my hotel and invited me back the next day I made some excuse but thanked them for their hospitality.

If you weren't on duty you didn't go near the boat so three days later when it was my turn to do a duty I was amazed to see the gargantuan aircraft carrier USS George Washington berthed in front of us. I need to put this in context on the surface HMS Triumph displaced 4,740 tons, the USS George Washington displaced 104,200 tons, Triumph had a crew of 130 and the George Washington had approximately 5,680 give or take a few, when the air wing was embarked and they were. It towered over us like the spaceships in the film Independence Day. We had some visitors from the US ship and asked them who many they had on duty when alongside, they told us just over 600, we had 8. It was pointless asking their duty watch for a 'call round' we couldn't fit them on board! We were asked if we wanted shown around their ship but we had to refuse we only had 5 days left in port and it would have taken a week for us to get round the top four decks alone. They even had one sailor whose job was to maintain the coke machines on board. They had nearly as many laundry 'assistant mates' than we had crew.

In fact they actually had more cooks that HMS Triumph had crew, had an American football league with three teams and such luxuries as McDonalds, Pizza Hut and Taco Bell as well. It really was a floating city and reportedly the Captain had a permanent escort of 4 US Marines. They were still a target and a big one at that, if the USS Baton Rouge was protecting her she was in the shit, unless she was attacked by Buffalo wings.

We completed our R&R and once more stored the boat.

All ships and submarines have cocktail parties when in port or 'cock and arse' parties as they are known, at one of these events in Fort Lauderdale a young rating was told by a rather drunk but gallant Naval Officer to "take these young ladies home" so he did, he was away for three days as the young ladies were actually on holiday in Fort Lauderdale, so he drove them the 400 miles home! He ended up in RN

Detention Quarters (DQs) as Triumph had sailed for another exercise and destination, Cape Canaveral, before he got back. The next exercise involved another French ship and another US Submarine; we killed the frog but missed the yank.

We were heading for Cape Canaveral, the home of NASA and the Space Shuttle. We arrived at the facility and berthed safely and headed off to our hotels, which were in Coco beach. I was able to duck the ordeal of "Dial a Sailor"; Rick O'Connor had put me off the idea of being temporarily adopted. One thing we did get sorted very quickly at Coco Beach was that they had a soccer team, so a match was on the cards. We played a junior league team and they humped us, it was the weather, the heat was on their side. The local Royal Navy Liaison Officer had sorted out discounted tickets for all the Florida attractions; the 8 days in lower Florida were going to be the holiday of a lifetime. We bought tickets for the lot the Epcot centre, Universal Studios, Wet 'n Wild', Busch Gardens, Sea World and of course Disneyland. In true submariner fashion we 'zapped' every site. That's to say that we applied small foam backed copies of the boats plaque to various rides and locations through the theme parks. I went back to Universal studios some years later and our 'zapper' was still there! Our Army guest from the Devon and Dorset left us, but not before announcing the following:

"I was told before I joined this submarine, that submariners were undisciplined and unprofessional . . . . gentlemen it has been a pleasure to be your guest, you are all highly professional". The plank had forgotten to also mention that we were also highly disciplined, you have to be on a submarine or someone ends up getting hurt. Typical 'Pongo' as the Royal Navy and Royal Air Force called the Army.

CHAPTER 14

Back to Blighty and beyond

The US trip was great as for many of the crew it was their first time in the states, and we had certainly contributed to the US economy, there were bloody golf clubs stowed all over the boat, they were cheaper in the states. We were now homeward bound, no pretend wars just a straight sail home to Plymouth and the rain. We arrived in the early hours of the morning and went straight onto a buoy in Plymouth sound; it was cheaper for the RN to wait until after 09:00 instead of having to pay dockers overtime for working out of hours. So we hung about within sight of our home port lights and waited. We eventually got alongside our berth just before lunchtime and again F.O.H.S.B was announced and those of us not on duty went on leave.

When we returned from leave we had a spell in the attack trainer and done the usual courses and sports, and participated on the annual Navy Days Public relations event. We also had a short spell in dry dock for repairs and entertaining ourselves making prank phone calls whilst on duty. We would phone people who had placed adverts in the local newspapers and take the piss out of the advertiser, classics such as ringing the seller of a 'Burnt Orange carpet' to ask how badly burnt it was, when clearly burnt orange was the colour. Ringing the Naval dockyard tank cleaning department and asking how much it was to get a full valet and an air freshener for a Sherman. We would also take the mickey out of new joiners to the boat by asking them to make 'pipes' (RN for tannoy announcements) for fictitious persons such as RO Tate (Rotate) or WEM Brant (Rembrandt), asking them to report somewhere, we were easily pleased. We even had a visit from the local press and had fun with them, the next day one of the headlines read 'WRENs *hips too big for submarines*' this was because one of the crew had told the reporter that this was why there were no females on British submarines, one very unhappy Royal Navy press department, lots of unhappy WRENs and one chuckling submariner!

The next month or so was spent with crew going on courses, undertaking promotion exams, transferring to other boats, leave and going on the piss. The submarine service is a surprisingly small community and generally with each squadron many people will know and will have served on different boats with each other, as such 'legends' and 'dits' (Royal Navy term for stories) emerge and are shared. Crews are very close and some of the language overheard by 'outsiders' would probably offend, but within context it is not offensive. One such story is of a boat receiving a new crew member who shouted down the main access hatch into the control room:

"Have you any niggers on this boat?"

The shocked sailor in the control room confused by the outrageous question replied:

"No"

Only to have the new crewman jump down into the control room throw his arms apart and wriggled his hands like a vaudeville star of old and announced:

"You have now", he was non white.

It was his way of breaking the ice and out of context would have proved to be very offensive as the N word is thankfully no longer acceptable in our tolerant society.

During one of the regular periods of duty on the casing of a submarine I was joined, briefly by the duty sailor (who I will mention later) from the boat alongside us, he pointed at another boat and stated:

"I'm glad I not on that shit heap",

"Why?" I asked

"Because all my kit is on this one" . . . . caught again.

But that was submariners; you always had to be on your guard for the practical joke as it was never too far away. On another occasion a sailor was on the casing and took one pace to the rear in preparation to salute dignitaries that were boarding the boat, he stepped back too far and slid off the boat into the harbour, no immediate help was available as the crew were too busy laughing, maybe not such a big issue but the boat was in Stavanger, Norway in November and the water was freezing, he was recovered and put in a warm shower fully dressed until his blue skin turn pink again and he stopped shivering.

We set to sea for a week to participate in some further exercises to keep us sharp knowing that we should soon be told we were to go on deployment again. These exercises were slightly different as we practised a lot of 'boat transfers', helicopter working and on one occasion taking the boat down to her maximum diving depth to test some additional equipment that had been installed. Back alongside. On a run ashore I got into a stupid wrestling match with a local and ended up breaking my wrist, I was immediately medically downgraded (P7RD as the Navy call it) and made unfit for sea, I was gutted as Triumph had just received operational orders the day previously, she was now going to the Mediterranean and I wasn't, she was away for 4 weeks, stopping off in Gibraltar on the way. Her task was to document the approaches to and the ports of, a specific country. Television has shown the world that, which was and still is the sort of tasking that a submarine can undertake. A NATO ally of the UK actually sold a ship to another nation then spent millions of pounds having to deploy a submarine to get the acoustic signature of the vessel. Before Triumph sailed I applied for more leave and was granted it, 7 days leave and two days travel time, when I went to the squadron office to inform them of my 9 days leave they also added two days travel time . . . 11 days off for the price of 7 . . . . bargain.

Upon my return I was ordered to start work in the squadron offices. I returned from my leave to find that I was working alongside another submariner, a Geordie lad who, even by submariners standards, was nuts. We had a rather nice looking female Officer working in the squadron and my Geordie pal had noticed that every day she would turn up at her office and that some time during the day she would lick a handkerchief and polish he desktop name badge then lick it again and polish once more. For a couple of days he would watch her do this and then go into fits of laughter and none of us knew why. It was only later we found out that each night he would masturbate over the desktop badge and let it dry. She was polishing off his semen daily and didn't know it.

My new colleague was constantly annoying a certain Petty Officer who had had enough and eventually told him to "Fuck off" so he did, for 9 days. He was finally sent to RN DQs for 14 days after standing naked on a boat in the Old Barbican Harbour, as you would expect some good citizen called the police. When the police arrived, he turned and faced them saluted, dived into the harbour and swam to the other side. He climbed aboard another boat. The police officers ran to the other side of the harbour and as they stared to descend some harbour steps he repeated the evolution in the opposite direction and this continued with an ever growing and cheering crowd until enough police arrived on scene to cover both sides of the harbour at which time he was arrested and handed over to the Naval Shore Patrol. He soon became a legend, albeit only in and around the Barbican.

The same guy had learnt a trick from another submariner, who had been within him through recruit training, seamanship and submarine training parts 1 and 2. This involved them visiting a very popular high street Pizza chain and sitting down to starters, huge main courses, deserts and of course beer. They would not rush; they would be pleasant and courteous with the staff and generally be model customers. Following the dessert they would order a carafe of wine as soon as the waiting staff were not looking they would pour either salt, vinegar or sometimes lemon juice, that they had brought with them, into the wine one would make himself sick and the other would run to the toilet. The staff generally panicked and rushed to their aid, full of apologies and wondering how could the two pleasant and well mannered young men have taken ill so quickly. The two submariners would point out that the wine was 'corked' and tasted disgusting, the staff would taste it and agree, more often than not they got a huge discount, sometimes even free and vouchers to come again! It only worked on a specific location once, but allegedly it did work all over the world.

Triumph returned from her trip with her casing covered in fish hooks! During her patrol she had been in shallow waters and had inadvertently transited through an area were the natives were fishing by using hand lines and simply drifting, no noise, no target! The locals must have worn themselves out when trying to haul HMS Triumph to the surface. At one point the periscope was raised to find two native fishermen in a small wooden boat pointing at the periscope, clearly both frightened and confused. Like the many tales of fishermen all over the world, I bet nobody believed this story when they got home.

The next proposed trip for Triumph would be a world beater, she was scheduled to travel to Simonstown, (South Africa), Singapore, Perth (Australia) and then home via the Suez canal, which would mean that she was scheduled to travel over 40,000 miles without any support. This would be the longest solo deployment by any British nuclear submarine and it would also be the first time that a nuclear submarine, of any nation, had transited the Suez Canal, South to North. The crew knew she was a great boat, with a great Captain, and the world, in addition to all the Helensburgh taxi drivers, would soon know it also.

CHAPTER 15

To the Gulf and Beyond

The sailing orders for Triumphs 'world tour' came through and they were slightly amended. We were to leave Plymouth, sail to the Persian Gulf, across the Indian Ocean, the through the Malacca Straits, stopping of at Abu Dhabi, Diego Garcia (a little known island at the time), Perth, Singapore, then home via the Suez Canal and the Mediterranean Sea. The logistics of such a trip must have been a nightmare for the Supply Officer and his staff, but that was his main job, the crew were ready and the boat was ready and at lunchtime we sailed.

We would not just be transiting to the exotic places on the trip profile we, as ever, would be exercising with various other nations from time to time. Our first dive out of Plymouth was not without incident and I must admit it was my fault, secrets don't last very long on boats believe me and if the crew are messed about they want to know who and why. We were dived and transiting as normal and the crew went about their routine duties, I was asked to go to the 'bomb shop' for something and as I climbed down the hatch into the bomb shop my backside caught on an telephone cable which stretched and somehow touched and set off a flood alarm! Next to fire the most dangerous and scariest thing a submariner can experience is flooding, believe me a hole in a submarine is not a good idea, the guys manning the control panel on any submarine do not have to ask permission to react to flood alarms, they make the unilateral decision to execute an 'emergency blow' based on the circumstances at the time, on this occasion the sailor operating the panel decided to 'blow', alarms went off all over the boat, people started bracing themselves for the journey to the surface and I tried to hide! The angle of ascent was reduced when it was realised there was no flood and everyone on the boat wanted to know who and more importantly why? I felt like a real prat, it was accidental, but it still cost me a case of beer in my mess, the Senior rates mess and the Ward Room. We continued our journey on the surface, in rough weather, on a positive note it gave the air tanks the chance to get replenished.

The next 'event' was planned meticulously and that was the 'crossing of the line' submarine style, as it is only submariners that can hypothetically go under the equator once that was done we altered course so we could do it on the surface. This ceremony has been in place since time immemorial and consists of those who have not 'crossed the line' being humiliated by those who have, but it's all good fun and you get a certificate at the end. The key players are as to be expected King Neptune and a cast of 'hangers on' such a fictitious policemen etc. The 'candidates' had to eat 'fat pills' a concoction that the crew had made, I am not exactly sure what the contents were and knowing submariners I didn't really want to know. What I did know was that there was a hell of a lot of Tabasco sauce or something similar as part of the ingredients as the inside of my mouth felt as if it was starting to blister, at least someone gave me a drink to try and sooth the burning, the only problem was it was soapy water and I just heaved up all over myself as my hands had been tied as part of the ceremony and I was half kneeling half lying down. Then we had to endure being painted with a brown liquid in which someone had either placed essence of shit in or, as is more than likely the case, someone had actually shit in it. Shortly afterwards we were granted 'hands to bathe' and leapt off the boat into the ocean, joined by our tormentors! Climbing back up the side of a submarine using a knotted rope is hard enough as the outer skin, which is covered in 'acoustic tiles', is very smooth and quite slippy. It becomes neigh on impossible when some arsehole decides to have some fun by adding washing up liquid into the equation, and that's what happened. It was like something out of a 'Carry on' film, real slapstick stuff, anyone lucky enough to meet the challenge and get aboard the boat would have to lie down on the casing to catch their breath. It seemed to take an age to get everyone back on board. The benefit of hands to bathe in this location was that we joined a very select bunch that had actually swum across the Equator both on the surface and symbolically underwater.

We continued our journey round the Horn of Africa towards Abu Dhabi both submerged and on the surface. Throughout the trip we would actively target every ship we came in contact with to ensure we didn't lose our combat edge, submarines are no different from any other branch of the armed forces, its practise, practise, practise, Remember—train hard, fight easy. We maintained our 6 on, 6 off routine and periodically would receive mail, via a Royal Navy helicopter. The crew had decided to raise money for charity by beating the mileage covered by Triumph on an exercise bike, now you may think this would be impossible and it probably would have been if we had not cheated. Those who had pledged money did not get ripped off; we actually did beat the mileage 'clocked up' by the boat, How? It was easy. When the boat was in port the duty watch would still be pedalling, so we would not only catch up, we would be ahead of the boat, which would in turn overtake the charity team when at sea. We arrived at Abu Dhabi. In the blazing heat, as to be expected for the Gulf region, we had been 'bronzing' on the casing when the opportunity arose but submarines are fully air-conditioned so whilst at sea you don't really get the chance to a acclimatise to the conditions. The boat was rigged for port and F.O.H.S.B was announced. I had received, what at the time was, bad news from home and the Royal Navy were ready to send me home, however I decided that there was no point in returning to the UK and gave up the chance to fly home, I ended up with a passport containing an exit visa from Abu Dhabi, but we never went through immigration when arriving so did not have an entrance visa, little did I know the grief this would cause me later!

On the way to our hotel we noticed bodies laying beside the road, on roundabouts in cars it was unreal and looked like the population of Abu Dhabi had been wiped out with some sort of weapon of mass destruction. It turned out that they were all having a midday kip due to the heat. It was my first experience of what I named the 'Bingo callers', the Mullahs calling the community to prayers. One of the ex pat community told me of a colleague who used to wait until the congregation had gone into the Mosque to pray and he would then swap their shoes around which would cause mayhem, particularly on a Friday. His employer sacked him for this potentially volatile practical joke; he could have been flogged at best if caught at worst, who knows. His British employer couldn't take any chances and as a nation the last thing we wanted at the time was the nation of Islam teaming up with the communist hordes!

Our hotel was great and the local staffs were impeccable. We stupidly arranged a football match with some ex-pats and had to stop after about half an hour as the Triumph team simply wilted in the heat. Due to the fact that Abu Dhabi is a Muslim country there are very few bars other than ex-pat clubs and hotels. Ex-pats all over the world get together for major sporting events and Abu Dhabi was no different and a crowd had gathered in the hotel bar to watch the Grand National. Unfortunately it was the year that the Grand National was a fiasco so we never saw it, by the end of the night many of us couldn't see anything. We stored the boat for sea with food and left Abu Dhabi. The first thing we noticed was that the sausages that we had brought on board were, well different, clearly being a Muslim country there was no pork sausages and what we ended up with was a 'form' of hotdog, they were horrible and I am sure I wasn't the only one on the boat who thought that. The rest of the fresh provisions were good, but I still have a pathological hatred of hotdogs and Jon Secada, not as a person but his song 'Just Another Day' as his CD got stuck in the mess stereo and it was all we could listen to for about three weeks. We sailed for Diego Garcia a tropical, footprint-shaped Atoll in the middle of the Indian Ocean, again in the blazing heat. On the way we had a number of operational missions to conduct, which are probably still subject to the Official Secrets act so we'll leave them alone, apart from the fact that we listened and watched, and listened and watched. Most of the journey was submerged. Entering the Diego Garcia was a strange experience as we approached the Atoll the boats depth sounded was showing vast depths, and I mean thousands of feet, below us and as we approached and entered the Atoll the depth suddenly reduced to about 30 metres in minutes. The Atoll is part of the Chagos-Laccadive Ridge which is a vast submarine range in the Indian Ocean. I am not sure how deep it actually is or even if it is known, but it's bloody deep! The Atoll was owned by the British would bought it from Mauritius in the mid sixties so they could allow our American allies the opportunity to build a base there. The Americans never gave us any money for this prime piece of military real estate, but as a result of us letting them be our tenants they did give us a big discount when we bought Polaris missiles off them, barter international style! But there is still a token British presence in the form of Naval Party 1002 (NP 1002), a small detachment of Royal Navy and Royal Marine Commando personnel. Diego is strictly a military base with very few civilian residents and not hotels we had to stay in military accommodation, but we were in the Middle of the Indian Ocean so we could cope. First thing I noticed apart from the fact it was idyllic, was that there appeared to be lots of Donkeys! We were scheduled to stay for a week but due to some minor repairs we ended up staying for nearly two weeks. We were fed in the US military facilities, which meant steaks all day and when I say steaks I mean BIG ones, clearly when the buffalo's wings failed and they plummeted to the ground the US military picked them up, shaved them, cut the head off, wiped the arse and fried the bastards. There was also ice cream and coke on tap.

The sporting events were arranged and we played NP 1002 at football on a sand and shell football pitch, the marines wore combat boots, we wore football boots and the marines won! Royal Marines tend to be fitter than submariners and they were used to the heat, and eating huge steaks, that's my excuse and I'm sticking to it. The next sporting event was Softball, against a US/UK team from the base, it was really rounders for big boys, strangely when we played this it actually rained, proper tropical rain. The shower didn't last for more than 30 minutes but the raindrops were like golf balls, it was torrential but warm rain and the softball pitch was sodden within seconds, this time we had the advantage, we were from Britain we could do rain! It helped and we won, the sun had obviously made the US/UK Marines forget any arctic warfare or wet weather training they had done in the past, but I have to say the US Marines were more annoyed that we referred to one of their national sports as rounders! The island may be small but the cockroaches were HUGE, I remember seeing one in our accommodation and decided the terminate it so I stomped on the bugger only to have it appear look up at me as if to say 'is that all you've got' and then scurry away, I prayed for the rest of my stay that he hadn't gone to get his Dad or big brother, it was like a bloody skateboard with legs. We would spend days swimming in the lagoon and do Robinson Crusoe type things like pick up conch shells and coconuts until we realised that there is such a thing as a coconut crabs and that within the three weeks previously there had been a US serviceman attacked by a hammerhead shark. You would have thought that someone would have told us that on the day we arrived. Our US colleagues offered some of us the opportunity to go fishing and a number of the lads took up this kind offer and off they sailed out of the lagoon in a small sports fishing boat. When they returned there was a massive shark hanging half in and half out of the boat. They clearly had a good time, we sat down with them to watch the video of the catch to see that they had brought this beast to the surface and it was somewhat annoyed thrashing and writhing all over the place. The video showed three British sailors trying to distance themselves from the business end of the shark, that I am sure in their time of terror appeared to be as big if not bigger, as the small boat they were on, whilst shouting to the US sailors to:

"Just let the fucker go"

The two US sailors were shouting at their British colleagues:

"We can't let it go, it's tied to the boat, fucking help you stupid bastards,"

Sheepishly three Brits started to apprehensively hang onto the line with one of the yanks whilst the other disappeared into the wheelhouse only to return with a 9mm Browning pistol and subsequently emptied it into the shark, it eventually lay still. We writhed about in hysterics. We spent pounds in the various bars, in particular the 'Brit bar' and bought Hawaiian style shirts in the few shops that were on the island, one or two of us also learnt never to play poker with Americans. We stored the boat, set for sea and sadly said farewell to the Footprint of Freedom, as Diego Garcia is known.

CHAPTER 16

Australia here we come

The next port of call for the mighty 'T' was HMAS Stirling, in Rockingham, Western Australia. This Naval Base is the Australian Navy's main Fleet Base and the home of Australian submariners and it has its own SETT. It is also the home of Clearance Diving Team 4, who are seen by themselves as an 'elite' bunch. The journey to Australia was not uneventful, HMS triumph, whilst dived, suffered a 'full positive earth' to skimmers and landlubbers that means she blew a fuse and a big one at that. We had a period when the boat clearly had a 20-30 degree angle and the depth counter was going up, in other words we were slowly sinking deeper, albeit stern first. The engineering staffs on the boat were manic and the rest of the crew just lay down, you use a lot less oxygen when you're lying down saying prayers. The Black Hand gang eventually got the thing working and with a huge sense of relief we headed to a more acceptable and less scary depth. The poor sole that caused it was subject to military discipline, enough said. Like all sailors, in fact men, stupid wagers were set on the trip to Australia, most involving either beer, football or women. One such bet saw a particular crewman wager every member of the mess, a case of beer each, that he could bed the first female that spoke to him upon arrival in Australia, needless to say because of the standards he had set himself in other ports this was no long shot. But being bored many accepted the wager, the only caveat was that it did not have to be on the day he met her, just before we left Australia, which gave him 10 days. We arrived first thing in the morning; Australian dockyard workers are not bothered that it's before 09:00, as their Navy can afford the overtime and the boats was secured alongside. F.O.H.S.B. Just as leave had been announced the sailor in question was called to the control room to meet his cousin Julia who was in the Australian Navy!! Legend has it, that he offered to share half the beer with her, but she drank wine, so declined this kind offer.

Our hotel for this trip was in Perth and the news had got out to the local ladies that we were staying there, it also became apparent that the information had also found its way to a few of the local arseholes. It turned out that the latter couldn't box eggs let alone submariners! Once the arseholes learnt the hard way that the crew of HMS Triumph could be very protective of each other, they chose to pester some other poor sods, street cred with the ladies. We took the opportunity to do the touristy thing and visited a number of 'attractions', and go and see a game of 'Aussie Rules' football. It appeared that we didn't only send criminals to Australia but also all the nutcases, the guys that play that game are in a word, MENTAL. Let's hope they didn't want to play us at their national sport, rain, shit or shine we would have been destroyed. The trip was interspersed with the usual duties and we would get 'call rounds' from Australian submariners and they would repay the hospitality, during one of these visits we had been told of one of the many things, which reside in Australia, that want to bite you. I have always lifted toilet seats since that briefing. We were also advised of other 'things' that looked scary but were harmless, one of these was the Huntsman spider which we were told, always hung about in pairs, could get quite large but were harmless and the bite, although not fatal, was 'extremely uncomfortable'. Some Australians apparently like them because they kill cockroaches. The attitude was quite cavalier, but understandable, given that many other things, some of which were very small and coloured red wanted to either make you very ill or kill you. Too make matters worse some actually chose to hide under lavatory seats, maybe that's why I now always leave the toilet seat up?

One evening whilst on duty a colleague and I were patrolling the casing and dockside in turn, when something moved in the shadows and caught the corner of my eye. I told my colleague who joined me to investigate and hiding beside a pile of wood on the dock was not so much a spider but a bloody transformer, it was gigantic. It raised its two front legs in defence which was enough to scare the shit out of both of us, even though we were armed. As we stepped away from the beast, keeping an eye on it, we simultaneously had the same thought: 'Where's the other one?' and then simultaneously set off at a pace to get back on board the boat. We had a 15-20 minute debate as to whose turn it was to guard the dockside and agreed that nobody would steal Australia, so we doubled up on the casing. During our stay we were invited to of a barbeque by the crew of an Australian submarine; it was Australia I'd have been really pissed off if we hadn't got to a real Aussie Barbie. During this event, at which we had to wear uniform, we had all the usual stupid games and drinking challenges and things were going great until a member of Clearance Diving Team 4 (CDT) turned up. I now know that Aussie submariners don't like their own CDTs, however this guys was an ex RN sailor and he thought that he would be Ok turning up at the submariners Barbie, wrong. He also thought that he was Ok because he was an ex RN member, wrong, submariners stick together. It was getting quite hostile and he wouldn't leave and was ready to start on the Aussies when I took him to the side and asked him to leave, he told me he'd have to be thrown out . . . . so I threw him out, to the cheers of the Aussies. We carried on and had a damn good time. The following morning the Officer of the Day (OOD) took me to task, made a mountain out of a molehill and accused me of trying to start what he considered could have been an 'international incident', I had stopped a bloody row not caused it. A few days later I was caught doing 45km in a 40km area on the base and an Aussie Naval policeman pulled me over, thinking I was in deep shit I tried to get away with a pleasant awkward smile. It was never going to work. He wandered over to the hired minibus and immediately noticed I was a British sailor:

"You off that, Pommie sub?" he asked

"Yes" I replied

"You were speeding mate" he said

"Was I, I didn't realise" I replied

"You were doing 48km, what speed does it say on that road sign?" he asked pointing at a nearby sign

"40km" I answered

"Good, nothing wrong with your eyesight, now just because it has a sign on either side of the road doesn't mean you can go at 80km" he remarked sarcastically.

"Ok, got that" was my answer

"Did someone off your sub, do a diver over?" he asked and I thought oh shit I'm now going to get done with assault.

"Yes, I believe so, he was asked to leave a barbeque and when he refused, he was thrown out" I answered

"Well you buy him a beer on me" he said and then walked away.

As is required I got back to the boat and reported my near misdemeanour to the OOD who retorted that "This just isn't your trip", how right he was. I stayed on board and facilitated some visitor and then had a few beers in the mess, we were being cleared off the boat to make way for a cock and arse party and the OOD was quite abrupt, I stupidly let the beer take over and told him in front of other sailors and visitors that he couldn't lead a mayday parade let alone a bunch of sailors and that he was a wanker. For the first time in my military career I was disciplined or trooped as the Navy call it. I was charged with insubordination and given into the custody of the Royal Australian Navy Police. The guy that was in charge of the party that drove me to the base cells was the very same cop who had stopped me for speeding earlier. I arrived at the cells and they left the door unlocked and the duty watch even brought me pizza.

The next day I appeared in front of the Captain and the issue regarding the clearance diver was also raised by my charging officer and feared I would end up in DQs, but thankfully an Aussie Officer who had trained with our Captain was able to give the correct version of events to the accusing Officer and he was not happy that he got the wrong end of the stick and was a bit pissed off to say the least. I ended up getting 4 days restricted on board, in other words the rest of my trip to Australia, less two days, would be spent on the boat, bummer. Now we all know that positives come out of adversity. Well this occasion was no different rumours started to circulate HMAS Stirling and by the time it had travelled around the bazaars I had apparently hit the OOD; to the Aussies I was a hero. After one night at the hospitality of the Aussie Naval Police I was returned to Triumph to complete my 4 days 'restricted onboard'. The number of 'call rounds' to Triumph increased as lots of Aussie sailors wanted to meet the guy who chinned the OOD, this didn't help as the alleged victim of the fictitious assault was even more pissed off. The rest of the crew in my duty roster were chuffed to bits as I volunteered to pick up extra duties as I was not allowed off the boat. I was still given shitty jobs during the 4 days restrictions and not allowed to drink, but I was in my own sea rack and had periodic use of the mess between doing sentry duty and shitty jobs. My first day ashore after serving my punishment was all free beer, thanks to the Aussie submariners and I was able to meet a former military colleague from the past who had moved to Perth and whose son had joined the Australian Navy. Even one of the local ladies was impressed with my alleged antics! I tried to use as much on my remaining time in Perth to see the sights. I still regret the incident, though more for missing out on the sights of Perth and the fact that up until then I had never had any disciplinary action taken against me throughout my military career. It could only happen to me I think I must be the only person to have been 'Transported' to Australia on a submarine, but then again I did get to go home. Any guilt I had was short lived; we stored the boat for sea and sailed for Singapore.

CHAPTER 17

Singapore and home

Most of us departed Australia with lasting memories most were good, but some to say the least were not so good. Given the congested sea en route to Singapore most of our journey would be spent on the surface. This allowed us to see dolphins, some small sharks and at one point we were even accompanied by flying fish, which clearly had better wings than buffalos. The main occurrence with this passage was that a volcano erupted which we heard and we were able to see, from a distance, the plumes of ash ejaculating from it. We were sailing between Sumatra and Java, passing from the Sunda Straits into the Java Sea and the volcano was none other than Krakatau, which erupted cataclysmically in 1883 and was made famous by Hollywood in the film Krakatau East of Java. In the early afternoon we docked at Sembawang, Naval Base in, Singapore. This stay was for 12 days to allow for routine maintenance of the boat and some minor onboard repairs. Once the boat was secured it was F.O.H.S.B. and off to our hotel. The first thing that I became aware of was the humidity, it was stifling. We had the usual array of sports events set up against ex-pats and had identified a number of tourist sites to visit, such as the museum of the former infamous World War Two Prisoner of War camp at Changi, and the Commonwealth War Memorial. We settled into the hotel and made for the restaurant and bar to grab something to drink, eat and plan our stay. Taxis are available in Singapore but we had to try out the trishaws or as we named them the 'wicky wicky' men, these were migrant workers who would transport, mainly tourist, around Singapore on a tricycle rickshaw, hence the name trishaw. These guys worked for a pittance, slept in these things by the roadside and if you tipped them enough they would actually wait outside bars, shops etc. for you. The aim was to get the one with the most lights or even a battery operated stereo on and towards the end of the trip we would actually pay the drivers to race each other or large submariners would pay to go 'three times around the war memorial' which incidentally was uphill. The 'wicky wicky' men of Singapore were in for a 12 day bonanza and they did us proud, some of them actually hung around outside the hotel and they were never short of business. I am sure it we had offered enough they would have pedalled us up stairs to our rooms. Great fun, if you ever go there try it.

Strangely the hotel kitchens were on the third floor of the hotel, which incidentally, had its own shopping mall and a roof top pool. On one occasion a couple of the lads were leaving the second floor bar and entered a lift, which the catering staff had placed a trolleys of food, as there seemed to be an abundance of food, they took a trolley to their room and ate the food on the trolley, with some left they shared it with others who were now aware of the scrumptious feast available in room 403. It was only afterwards that we found out the trolleys of food were a buffet destined for an engagement party in a function room on the fifth floor. I don't know how or where the trolley was returned of even if it was, but it served to contribute to one of the best room parties I'd been at.

Our sporting calendar was pretty full with, football, rugby and cricket on the agenda. The rugby was the first event we participated in and there were a few injuries. It is alleged that submariners can break their bones more easily, due to a lack of vitamin D which is naturally gleaned from sunlight, I don't know what the statistics are for submariners getting injured, but it doesn't appear to be any more than any other person/ sailor. During the rugby match I was racing to pick up a ball, bent down and then felt a pain I never previously experienced or imagined in my life, I let out a scream and the medic came running over. I had bent to try and pick up the ball up when an opponent had simultaneously tried to kick the bugger into orbit. The result was that I hyper-extended my right thumb and it was now pointing in the wrong direction, if I had been thumbing a lift I would have ended up where I started from! The trainer for the other team plunged my hand into a bucket of cold water, grabbed my wrist and 'forced' my thumb back into place, the pain I experienced earlier had just been equalled. I inherited the 'Fan daby dozy' 'wind up' for a few days. You don't ask or expect sympathy on a submarine, if you want sympathy it's between shit and syphilis in the dictionary. I went to the local hospital for a scan and it was only stretched ligaments so I'd live, our medic gleefully informed me that in the UK this type of injury was known as 'Avimore Thumb'. Everyone else went back to the bar of the Singapore Cricket club, like the aftermath of many rugby matches silly games and naughty songs coupled with lots of alcohol was the order of the day. Events clearly got out of hand, in particular when there were naked members of HMS Triumph rugby team on site, the Steward of the club eventually had only one option available and that was to close the bar until things had become more gentile. Not unique for rugby clubs, but this was a Cricket Club who had prided itself on the reputation that the bar had only every been closed once and that was following the Japanese invasion in February 1942, amend that reputation to now read twice. Oh and the cricket match was cancelled! The next event was the football against a team of ex-pats, in which we were once more beaten; the only injury of the game was my pulling of my quad muscle. This meant I spent most of the match hobbling about, watching our opponents score. It was definitely the humidity! As soon as the match was finished it was out with the tins of beer and cigarettes, our post match regime was quite a surprise to the locals team.

Some of the crew had visited the world famous Raffles hotel to try the famous 'Singapore Sling'. When Singapore fell to the Japanese Army on February 15th 1942, the colonialists living in the colony gathered at Raffles and with that world famous British stiff upper lip sang "There'll always be an England" in a display of defiance towards the invaders.

Our oppos had told us how fantastic the hotel was and advised us that if we were intending to visit to watch out for the FBI on the door. We thought that someone important might be in residence and it was the American Federal agency, but it turned out to be the rather large doorman who was dressed in traditional Raj clothing. FBI? Well that stood for Fucking Big Indian. We also visited Bugis Village, which in the past was the location of all the bars and houses of ill repute, unfortunately it had now become a manufactured tourist attraction with an abundance of street restaurants and market stalls selling counterfeit goods, I bought four watches and was advised by a waiter that at least one of them would be knackered by the time I got back to my hotel. Best the wick wicky man pedals fast, I thought. I woke up one morning in my hotel room to find there were some new clothes neatly folded on the dressing table, confused I tried them on and they fitted, free clothes, bargain! I only became aware of how the clothes came to be in my room when I was checking out and the cost was on my bill. Singapore has numerous tailors and the mall connected to our hotel was packed with them, I had gone into one after a few beers got measured for trousers and shirts ordered two of each and gave my room number.

I had promised myself that I would take time to visit the site of the infamous Changi POW camp and along with two others took a taxi to the site, it was too far away even for the herculean attributes of a 'wicky wicky' man. The site itself and the exhibits were haunting and I felt something at that site that I have never ever felt, nor want to feel ever again, it can only be described as evil. I actually did feel that something bad had happened at this place and was moved by the testimonials of the former residents and the chapel of remembrance.

As ever we stored the boat for sea and we departed Singapore. We had an uneventful journey across the Indian Ocean, entered Gulf of Aden and then the Red Sea before making our way to the southern entrance of the Suez Canal. Our Egyptian pilot boarded and we sailed North through the Bitter Lakes exiting Port Said in to the Mediterranean Sea. The Suez is nicknamed the "Highway to India", for the crew of HMS Triumph it was the "Highway to home". An uneventful passage through the Mediterranean, apart from being informed that the Royal Navy would be making people redundant under a programme called 'Options for Change' and in Bosnia the former communist hordes were now fighting each other, probably because we had made friends with them and they had no one to fight with. We arrived back in Plymouth, lay up on a buoy in Plymouth sound overnight, and docked in Devonport the next day. Under options for change there would be major cuts and changes to the RN. One of those changes was to close HMS Dolphin as the submarine school and move it to Faslane, so the skimmers took it over. F.O.H.S.B still emblazoned walls, skimmers thought it meant, as before, Fall Out Harbour Stations Below, submariners had penned a new meaning—Fuck Off Home Skimmer Bastards! As the communist hordes didn't want to fight with anyone but themselves, I applied for redundancy and was successful, D230948M Thompson had left the submarine.

CHAPTER 18

Clyde and beyond

The crew of HMS triumph, like most of the Royal Navy were aware that redundancies were a likely outcome for the proposed 'Options for Change' programme, with this in mind I had sent a letter off from Singapore to the then Coastguard Agency, repeating my interest in becoming a Coastguard Officer. I was quite surprised when I had a letter awaiting me in Plymouth with an application form and some recruiting material enclosed. I returning to Northern Ireland prior to the completion of my discharge from the Royal Navy, and whilst there took the time to also visit the Belfast Maritime Rescue Sub Centre (MRSC) in Bangor, County Down to speak to the then District Controller. He gave me some valuable advice and suggested that I apply for a posting to his station; I completed the application form and sent it off. I was disappointed to be told that they would retain my application as they did not have any vacancies, but expected to be recruiting within the next 6 months. Three weeks later I was flown to Edinburgh for a pre-joining medical which I passed no problem. Two weeks later I was then asked to attend an interview at the Clyde Maritime Rescue Co-Ordination Centre (MRCC), in Greenock, I was the only applicant from Northern Ireland, so was pretty confident I would be successful. Ten days later I received a letter offering me a position with Her Majesty's Coastguard, yes another uniform. The only drawback was that my first posting was to be at Clyde MRCC another applicant from Port Glasgow, next to Greenock, had been posted to Northern Ireland! We tried to have our postings swapped but it was not to be. After a month the bloke that had been posted to Northern Ireland actually handed in his notice and left. He was a former soldier and his family did not want to move to Northern Ireland as the war that wasn't, was still ongoing.

During my discussions with the staff at MRCC Belfast I had been shown a task book that I would be expected to complete and was given some guidance as to what different types of 'evidence' to include in it. I decide during my relocating trip from Stranraer to Greenock to take photographs of prominent landmarks on the coastline to include in my, soon to be issued, task book, one of these was Turnberry Lighthouse on the Galloway coast. Access to the lighthouse is via the golf course and I pulled into the car park, grabbed my camera and made for the lighthouse. As I crossed the golf course I was called to stop by a gentleman, who quickly rushed over to me.

"What's you name Sir and what are you doing here?" He asked

"My name is Davy Thompson and I'm going to take a photograph of the lighthouse" I replied with a Belfast accent.

"Why?" he asked

"I've joined the Coastguard and I have to do this as part of my training" I replied.

"Show me some ID" he demanded

"I haven't any on me, look what's all this about?" I said

"I'm the Police Officer, I'll ask the questions" he replied

"Haven't you got your Coastguard ID on you" he asked

"I haven't got it yet" was my reply

"Where are you based?"

"Greenock" I said

"What's the telephone number" he asked

"I don't know" I answered sheepishly

"You don't know the number of where you work?" he was now as confused as I was.

"Well I haven't really started yet" I felt really stupid now

He then produced a radio mumbled something into it and said

"Ok, come with me"

With that we both set off in the direction of my car with me protesting all the way that I had done nothing wrong and asking why was it illegal to take photographs of lighthouses in Scotland? As we approached the car park a police car pulled in with the blue lights on, thankfully no sirens were sounding. I was placed in the back of the car and taken to Stranraer Police Station, becoming more confused and worried on the trip as I was still getting questioned. Upon arrival I was placed in a 'custody suite', when I went to school they were called cells. After a short time another police officer arrived and asked me all the usual questions such as who, why, where and then left. He returned said:

"Clyde Coastguard has never heard of you",

Well they would not have would they? I had decided to travel to Scotland on the Friday, stay with friends in Glasgow for the weekend, before taking up my new job on the Monday. The staff at Clyde knew there was someone starting on the Monday, but because of the shift pattern the watch who were on Friday night didn't know the name of the new start. After they let me phone Clyde, I was able to get the District Controller to ring the police and confirm that a David Thompson was joining the HM Coastguard on Monday. The police took me back to my car and I was able to eventually find my passport and they were content to let me go. The whole cause of the incident was that Prince Charles was due to visit Turnberry Golf Club and during the pre-visit security screening I had unknowingly got my car with Northern Ireland number plates onto the golf course, abandoned it and was walking round taking photographs. This had served to make the police nervous. I was relieved at least I wouldn't have to go through this ordeal for every lighthouse I photographed.

On Monday Moring I reported for work, 146699 Thompson entered the building. I was assigned to D watch with two other officers, one and ex Merchant Navy Officer and the other was a former Royal Navy Warrant Officer, who had served on diesel submarines and was at one time a member of the FOST staff. The ex Merchant Navy Officer was the designated, the Senior Watch Officer (SWO) for the watch. Both were extremely experienced officers, the SWO would prove to be an inspiration to me (thanks Dave), his knowledge and experience were invaluable to me throughout my on the job training. The training programme would be two months on station, six weeks at HM Coastguard Training Centre, 7 months on station and then I would be required to pass 9 professional Coastguard exams. Once the training was completed and the exams all passed you became 'established' and had a permanent job, until then we were under probation. I was given a task book and was not allowed to undertake any tasks until I had passed what is known as the VHF ticket, in other words until I proved that I was competent enough to answer marine band VHF radio distress, urgency, safety (DUS) and routine calls. I also had to undertake a typing test. The former RN Warrant Officer would ask me questions out of the blue, a few Coastguard questions but mainly about submarines.

"What did you do?" he would ask

"Tactical Systems" I would reply

"Where you always on nukes?" he said, enquiring further

"Yes" I replied

"Fucking poof"

He would refer to me as a FLUNOB, which stood for Fat Lazy Useless Nuclear Orientated Bastard, he didn't like nuclear submarines and I didn't like the 'FLU' element. He was very intelligent and quick witted, he would come on watch and complete the Times newspaper crossword in a ludicrously short time. His mode of travel to work was on a small 50cc motorbike which he called the 'Flying Flea' and he liked a drink. Clyde MRCC was within the confines of a Naval Establishment and like all military establishments it had a Guardroom and a barrier to manage access to the site, there was a small 1-2 foot gap between the barrier and the guardhouse. On one occasion my colleague came into the operations room dishevelled and with a bleeding arm and quickly filled in the accident book, his report was to the point, no frills, it read "Endeavoured to negotiate gap between barrier and guardhouse . . . . FAILED". My colleague was in the last months of his career and had started his run down period; evidentially this included having a pint on the way into work. One evening he was seen to be going, round and round a roundabout for approximately 10 minutes, holding all the traffic up until he eventually plucked up the courage to straighten up at which point he over compensated and fell off the Flying Flea, this event was observed by a couple of astounded policemen, and a number of drivers who were in stopped cars. Colleagues in the Police kindly rang us and told us he wouldn't be in that night. Upon starting his very last shift he announced that he would have a headache at 4pm and would be going home. Throughout the day he would 'nip out' to the locker room or toilet and it soon became obvious that he was taking a 'wee dram', so the Senior Watch Officer decided to send him home before his headache arrived. He prepared to leave and made his very last radio transmission to those he had been guardian to for so long:

"Whoever you are and wherever the fuck you're going have a safe journey this is the big bad Wolf, out" at least he didn't tag "This is Clyde Coastguard" on to the end of the message.

As part of my training I, like all trainee Coastguards, had to undertake local knowledge visits and one particular location was and remains 'legendary' for such visits and that was Islay, the island I had visited for R&R whilst with the RAF. Myself and two colleagues would soon be visiting the island to familiarise ourselves with the hazards, topography, RNLI crews and our very own Volunteer Coastguards. The latter are the community minded individuals who have normal 'day jobs' but are trained in how to conduct searches, Coastguard procedures and the use of various types of rescue equipment. In recent years they have seen equipment and training improve to a level that could only be dreamt of 20 years ago. One piece of equipment they previously used was the famous 'Breeches Buoy', this was in effect a pair of canvas 'breeches' sewn onto a lifebuoy, hence the name 'Breeches Buoy' this was a cumbersome set up and required a much greater number of volunteers that today's modern equipment. I recall a story of one volunteer who was invited to watch the local Coastguard Rescue Team (CRT) training as a prelude to joining the service. He watched intently as the CRT turned up at the scene and started to lay out the equipment under the guidance of the Full Time Sector Officer. The onlooker noticed they were very disciplined and reacted sharply to the barking orders from the Sector Officer. One particular element of the drill appeared to be causing some confusion and the Sector Officer made the CRT repeat the action on a number of occasions, as he became evidently frustrated with the way the evolution was being conducted. He suddenly announced:

"Right, enough is enough, get the whips out"

At this point the potential volunteer disappeared, it was only afterwards he found out that 'whips' were the name of the rope lines used in the drill and not a means of making the CRT improve its performance. He stilled joined. It is the volunteers who perform the actual rescue of individuals. These individuals give a huge amount of time, effort and commitment to HM Coastguard for very little remuneration and many CRT have seen generations of the same family as members, and this is particularly the case on the islands surrounding Scotland. It is not uncommon to see volunteers with 20 or 30 years service and a number even have 40 years service, that's longer than some marriages. I have always seen these individuals as colleagues and not just volunteers.

My colleagues and I got off the ferry at Port Ellen and made our way to the hotel; we grabbed a bite to eat then went straight to meet a CRT on the island who were training. After the introductions and the training event we all returned to the hotel, it appeared that, like the military, both the RNLI and Volunteer Coastguards adopted pubs and hotels as their own. Like my colleagues, I had no chance of keeping up with these hardy islands folk and they knew it. Just prior to the landlady announcing last orders a cry of "Take him round the island" went up followed by cheering and clapping from everyone on the bar.

My first thought was shit I had seen some of the smaller roads and there was no way I was getting into a car to take a trip around Islay at night with any individual who had been drinking and they all had. How the hell was I going to get out of this, my colleagues seemed unnerved they had obviously experienced such a road trip in the past and survived, but their survival shortened the odds for me, I was worried? Much to my relief a tray with 9 glasses on was placed on the bar and I was ushered towards it with the clientele chanting. Each glass had whisky in it and I never drink shorts, but it was better than the fearful drive I had imagined. The amount in each glass was larger than the previous glass across all 9. The significance of the 9 glasses was explained and it was because, at the time, there were still 9 working distilleries on the island, so a whisky from each one was presented, hence 'Going round the island'. When I enquired as to why the amount was increasing with each glass I was told "It's because the tides coming in", silly me. It was a tradition on the island to conduct this initiation on visitors, who the islanders thought would return as friends and Coasties certainly fell into that category. It certainly assured I had a good night's sleep. The next day we continued our familiarisation visit to the various coves and the volunteers highlighted the many areas with wrecks, hazardous tides and those sites which frequently would require and attendance by were very difficult to get to. This was so we, who after all be calling them out and co-ordinating their actions, had an idea of the difficulties they faced. Every island I have visited, and there have been many, the folk have been hardy and hospitable. I would visit Islay many times in both and official and leisure capacity. If you every get the chance to go to Islay, please go.

The main difficulty I had, initially, at Clyde was dealing with the Ayrshire accent, God knows how my colleagues faired on the East coast of

Scotland. One of the first messages I took was from a lifeboat and endeavouring to maintain the high standards required by my SWO on one occasion I asked him:

"How many Fs are there in Giffen?"

"What?" he asked

I repeated the question

"I have no idea, why do you want to know that?" he enquired

"Because I want to make sure I've spelt it right when I put it in the system that the Lifeboat is back and ready for service"

After some head scratching and replaying the voice recorder I got my answer, none, Girvan lifeboat was refuelled and ready for service. I felt a twat. Those first two months were spent learning to understand the Ayrshire accent and preparing to attend HM Coastguard Training centre at Highcliffe in Dorset, with another trainee from Clyde, who had joined two weeks before me. This would be our initial training as Coastguards and I wondered what recruit training would be like in civvy street.

CHAPTER 19

Highcliffe and beyond

I was provided with a hire car and set off on a bright Sunday morning with my colleague following in his own car for the 10 hour drive to Highcliffe; along with another trainee we had rented a house for the six week duration of our 'New Entry' course. We arrived in the sleepy hollow of Highcliffe, Dorset around 10pm and eventually found the house in question. We began to unpack our cars and were conducting trips to and from the house when my colleague announced that he had locked his car keys inside his car. I finished unpacking my hire car and he and the other trainee went to look for something to help gain access to his vehicle. I returned to his car and as all three of us were trying to get into his car an elderly gentleman approached us and asked what we were doing, we explained and he left, shortly afterwards the Police arrived. The gentleman had seen three males, who he did not know gathered around a car trying to get into it and one of the males was non white to boot, it was to him a crime in progress, welcome to Highcliffe. With the help of the police we eventually got into the car, retrieved the keys and unpacked it, all under the gaze of our new neighbours behind their twitching curtains. They would undoubtedly keep a close eye on us over the next six weeks. I was sitting in a pub having lunch, with colleagues, in Highcliffe one Sunday when a small boy pointed to me and asked his Grandmother what the marks on my arms and legs were:

"Tattoos" she replied to the inquisitive youngster

"What do they mean" he further enquired

"It means he's probably been in jail" was her answer and she didn't whisper.

I corrected her and told the young lad "Your Grandma is silly, some people collect stamps, some collect other things, I had these done in various places around the world" he giggled, she frowned and I ate my lunch.

Highcliffe has an aging population and very few retail outlets other than estate agents, opticians, mobility shops, charity shops, funeral directors oh and a Sainsbury's. The standing joke was that the Highcliffe Marathon was advertised as starting 10 am Sunday 4th April ends . . . . December. It is the only place I know of, that raised a petition to close a nursery, because it was too noisy and half the residents couldn't hear.

We reported to the training centre and were introduced to the rest of our course, in total 12 students consisting of 9 (including me) former RN personnel, 2 ex soldiers and an ex Merchant Navy 2nd mate. The first thing that hit me was the guy who had wagged me about his kit being on another submarine was on the same course. So out of the 9 ex RN two were submariners, one was an ex pilot, so that left 6 skimmers, I could handle that. Our instructors were all ex merchant Navy. We were to be known as NE 83. Throughout the six weeks we would complete training on maritime communications, search planning, search and rescue principles and procedures, meteorology and coastal rescue equipment and techniques. We quickly gelled as a course and made friendships, with other students, which have lasted to this day. We were all reasonably intelligent individuals and the course content did not appear to be causing us many difficulties and this resulted in a healthy social element to the course.

HM Coastguard Training Centre had no on site accommodation so when attending a course coastguard would traditionally stay in the local bed and breakfast establishments, the site did however have a canteen, which would provide lunches, at a small cost, for staff, trainees and visitors. This was an independent venture and has been run by various characters over the years the proprietor during our course was an elderly lady who we referred to as either "Lumpy Legs" (due to her varicose veins) or "The Soup Dragon". She did us proud though and despite the nick names, which we never used in front of her, we all grew quite fond of her and her of us. We ordered packed lunches prior to a trip off site to conduct cliff training and she mentioned those dreaded words to me "Do you like peanut butter?" I nearly had an anxiety attack before answering no. What is it with pensioners and bloody peanut butter? I think it is something to do with the yanks being over here during the war I am sure they brought here with them and elderly ladies are reminiscing about some youthful love affair they had. Those staying in B&Bs would normally eat out at night but because we had rented a house and cooked, we would normally have CG visitors and they would uncannily arrived around teatime during the week and at lunchtime over the weekend! One of my housemates was originally from Iraq and showed me how to cook rice properly; the other benefit of his cultural background was that he didn't drink so we had a permanent taxi driver. One night he took us to a local nightclub called the Highlander IV, we called it the HIV club, and no further description is needed. Late one night when we tried to get in one of our group as wearing trainers and refused entry so we hatched a cunning plan, one of us would enter the club go to the toilets and drop shoes out of the window for the trainer wearing colleague to wear and gain entry. The first part of the plan worked a treat, however with the intake of alcohol it proved difficult for us to throw trainers back up to the window for our 'inside man' to put on. We tried for about 15-20 minutes, only giving up when one of the trainers missed the target by yards and went over a wall. So we fell about laughing, in particular at the swearing toilet window, before going into the club with one of us spending the night drinking and dancing in his socks.

Towards the end of our course we arranged a barbeque for ourselves, other trainees, our instructors, senior officers from our HQ and all their families. It was all set up for our last Sunday and we all chipped in to buy lots of beer and food. On the day the weather was fantastic and a good crowd turned up and we soon got into the swing of things. We had 45 gallon drums filled with cold water and cans of beer and the barbeque was lit, we encouraged some of the instructors' children to soak senior officers with their water pistols and watched as their Dads tried restore their careers and try to calm them down, the children that is not the senior officers. During these antics all the burgers were knocked off a table and fell to the ground, they ended up covered in grass which we tried to brush off. The wife of a senior officer arrived at the barbeque and requested a burger for herself and her child, she immediately asked "What is that on the burger?" only to be told, by the quick thinking Coastguard chef, "Herbs", she slapped on the ketchup and went away none the wiser. It was approaching dusk went the barbeque started draw to an end as some of our guests were preparing to leave the whole of NE83 ran to the main gate and as our guests were leaving we 'mooned' at them, our Iraq colleague trained his car headlights on to the row of lily white arses just so our guests wouldn't miss anything. At the time we thought it was funny, this wasn't the view taken by our instructors, the senior officers, their wives and our female HQ colleagues. We were still on probation, so we dwelt on our feat overnight, the next morning we were told as a class that our careers were over! We quickly got flowers sent to our offended female colleague in HQ, by lunchtime we had received a pardon and thank you from her, and she also wanted to know which one of us had the tattoo on his bum? That was news to us we were all bent over so didn't know who it was let alone that someone had one, the culprit would let us know who he was but not until we returned in 7 months time for our finals. Our chivalrous move had saved our careers and we carried on with training. The final week passed without event or issue and we all prepared to return to our stations to start to develop the foundation skills we had either learnt or enhanced over the past six weeks. Throughout our training we were reminded that we needed to get out of what had become known as 'Bunker Mentality'. This effectively was telling us we needed to get out of our stations as often as practically possible and interact with our partners and the great British public. Maybe not significant at the time but in later years the purveyor of this mantra would appear to have a complete reversal of opinion.

CHAPTER 20

Clyde and beyond part 2

I returned to Clyde to complete my task book and prepare for my final exams 7 months later. This was on the job training when there were quiet periods I would complete training exercises and mock exams, in between I would carried out normal duties and deal with incidents under the guidance of my SWO. The 7 months flew in and I successfully passed the required exams to become an established Civil Servant. On the journey home with my colleague I overtook two Lorries on the M6 as I passed the forward of the two lorries I suddenly realised there were blue flashing lights in my rear view mirror. I pulled onto the hard shoulder and a figure exited the Police car came to the driver's window and invited me to join him in his vehicle. The conversation with the Traffic Officer went as follows:

"What is the registration of your vehicle?" asked the officer

"I don't know, it's a hire car" I replied

"Can I see your driving license?"

"I haven't got it on me"

"How did you hire a car with no license?" he enquired

"My employer, hired it on my behalf"

"You were doing 94 miles an hour" he stated

"Sorry" I whimpered

"Can you take your license into a Police Station in England or Wales within the next seven days?" he asked

"Not really, I live in Scotland and my licence was a Northern Ireland license that I have sent off to get exchanged for a GB license" I replied

"You're taking the piss" was his reply

"I'm not" I answered

"My shift is finishing and I haven't got time for this shit, you're the luckiest driver on the M6, now bugger off" He groaned

"Are you sure" I stupidly asked

"Yes, now bugger off before I decide to change my mind" he snapped

"Ok have a good day" I said, I immediately cringed at my answer and returned to the hire car.

Now was the time to consolidate what I had learnt in the past 10 months and become a real Coastguard. Many Coastguards will remember details of the first time they dealt with a fatality, it is really something that does not leave you, and it would not be right or dignified to talk about such events. But there are a myriad of humorous tales from around the coast of the UK, probably enough to write a book on that subject matter alone. Watch this space.

I recall an event when a member of the public had rang 999 to report a yacht drifting with what looked like a person prone on the deck. The duty watch duly tasked a lifeboat and a CRT to respond, as the lifeboat approached the yacht it was clear to them that the person on board the boat was trying to hide from them and that the boat was aground and going nowhere. They eventually convinced the individual to come ashore with them which he reluctantly did, on arrival in a marine he was met by the CRT so they could get further details. The CRT gathered details and one volunteer prompted the other:

"Ask him what LSA (Life Saving Apparatus) he had on board"

Before the question could be asked the scruffy mariner retorted "Tell him I don't smoke that shit" they clarified matters whilst trying not to piss themselves laughing and remain professional. It turned out that he believed the police were harassing him so he had swapped a motor vehicle for the yacht, which had no charts or safety equipment, and he was sailing to Ireland to make his fortune. He had covered half a mile of his journey when he came to grief. The reason the Police were 'harassing' him was that his motor vehicle was neither taxed, MOT'd or insurance, because he was a New Age traveller and such things were against his principles. When his yacht was repaired we had to help him again.

On another occasion a fishing vessel called Clyde Coastguard to report something in his nets:

"Clyde Coastguard this is *******, I have a dead seal in my nets"

"******* This is Clyde, can you tell us where you are bound for and we'll pass that to the SSPCA" asked the operator

"Clyde, best you get the American Embassy, it's one of theirs" replied the fishing boat, the operator was gobsmacked.

The vessels crew had recovered, what they believed to be, the remains of a US serviceman that had been lost some years previous. They were thankfully wrong. Fishermen are like that most are as cool as cucumbers under pressure and very often the tone of their voices will not indicate any sort of emergency. I had a call from a fisherman once and all he said was:

"Clyde Coastguard this is ******* we're in a bit of bother and are getting into our life raft" that was it, no position no other information. After interrogating to get all the relevant information he simply said:

"Aye Clyde, we'll just wait on the lifeboat" no panic all very matter of fact, I was more scared that the crew.

I once took a call from the representative of a film company asking if I could get a ship to move from its anchorage as they were filming a period drama and the ship was in their shot, I explained that it was not a simple as asking the ship to move the caller asked me if I could not just tell him to move I said no. I gave the caller the details of the ship and her owners. A few hours later the ship called to say they were moving to a different position, now I wonder how much that cost? Upon answering a 999 call to report a red distress flare one of my colleagues asked the caller all the usual questions when he got to final question and asked:

"Have you any idea where the flare originated from"

Only to be told by the caller:

"Yes the boat that is on fire!" he had not thought to report the boat in the first instance.

A colleague was once asked:

"Does the Coastguard control the tides around Arran",

"No God does that" was his reply

"In that case, can you ask him what time High water is" was the caller's comeback.

I was selected to represent HM Coastguard at a Royal Garden party at the Palace of Holyroodhouse, as someone who had spent a lifetime in uniform this was a great honour. I was also allowed to be accompanied by my wife and I was given permission to stay overnight. On the day of the event we travelled to Edinburgh, the weather was superb, my wife had bought a new hat and dress and I had blisters on my index finger from bulling my shoes and less wrinkles on my forehead due to standing over a steam iron for so long, medals polished, haircut the effort that went into preparing for the event was enormous. We, excitedly, handed over our invitation at the entrance and were directed to a specific area were we would line up in preparation for an audience with her Majesty. There were also representatives from the other three Emergency Services, the Armed forces and Civic dignitaries. We formed parallel lines and anxiously awaited the arrival of the Monarch and her entourage. It had been pointed out to us that generally Her Majesty would look towards those she wished to speak to and this would give us an indication that she was about to come and speak directly to you. We were also reminded that the correct way to address the Queen is 'Mam' (must rhyme with jam). The Royal party eventually arrived after a short delay and the Queen and Prince Phillip began to interact with the assembled invited guests, stopping periodically to talk to individuals. As the party came closer to our location my wife was becoming ever more nervous and kept asking me what she was supposed to say if the party decided to talk to us, in an effort to calm her nerves I told her to relax and be herself. I had been told there was a very strong likelihood that the party would talk to us as the Monarch did not meet members of HM Coastguard very often; another factor was that HRH Prince Charles was the Honorary Commodore of HM Coastguard. Eventually the Royal Party approached us and Her Majesty looked directly at my wife and I, if the organisers were correct we were about to speak directly to the Queen. My wife noticed we had been selected and was now shaking, the Queen stopped for a moment and spoke to Prince Phillip, immediately my wife nervously asked me:

"What do you think she has just said?"

Again in an effort to calm her nerves and with that well honed Thompson humour I said: "She's probably just noticed my Coastguard uniform and said to Prince Phillip . . . . Isn't that Davy Thompson over there?"

At which point my wife burst out laughing and the Royal Party walked past us and my wife had lost her chance to meet the Queen.

All forms of maritime communications come under the umbrella of the Global Maritime Distress and Safety System (GMDSS) and I had a particular interest in the details of the system so went to Glasgow Nautical College to gain an externally recognised qualification. At the time there was no recognised Coastguard qualification, as a result of this course I produced a 'national' PowerPoint presentation to help other Coastguards better understand all the systems and later was asked to participate in a project team to develop and design a course for Coastguard that would eventually be recognised externally. As a result of these efforts I was asked to represent the UK at a conference to be held at the Canadian Coastguard College, in Sydney, Nova Scotia I didn't need to be asked twice. I paid for my wife to accompany me and on 1st September we flew from Glasgow to Halifax, Nova Scotia. We arrived in Halifax and stayed overnight at a hotel near the airport, in the Hotel there were a number of Canadian Coastguard who had flown from the other side of Canada en route to their own college. We got talking and the subject of the onward journey to Sydney arose, I told my new friends we were flying into Sydney from Halifax and they all looked at me horrified and explained they were driving the long distance to the college. I asked why and was told "you'll see".

The following morning we passed through departures with 3 other people and were led out onto the runway, there would be loads of room on the plane I thought and we would probably have our own personal cabin crew for the duration, given that there were so few passengers. I could see the nice shiny aircraft in the distance and we started towards it, to my horror we never reached the Air Canada 737, we had stopped at a small 8 seater aircraft. A small cart turned up with our baggage and we were asked to help the loader by passing the cases through the only door, from which they were packed at the back of the aircraft and a curtain draw to hide them. Apprehensively my wife and I boarded what looked like a bloody Airfix model and sat in our seats, the pilot turned round and told us how long the flight would be, no PA announcement he just shouted over the engine noise to the petrified group who had just embarked. The door was shut and I noticed there was no co-pilot, we taxied down a runway and took off, the adventure had begun. The flight appeared to be 'nap of the earth' flying as it was like being on a rollercoaster up, down, up, down and we appeared to be inches above the trees. It seemed like he had a contract with the Canadian forestry commission to take the tops off the trees during the journey, worst still it was a variable pitch propeller aircraft and we could hear the engine screaming and whining as he increased and decreased the throttle and the propeller pitch changing. I thought at one point that the bloody thing had a gear stick and he was having trouble getting it into gear. All the passengers were gripping something in the belief that the harder they squeezed the better the flight would be, it didn't work. Suddenly the aircraft appeared to scream at full revs and we thankfully gained height my relief was short lived the pilot then turned around, hands off the joystick, and passed a thermos flask, paper cups and a packet of Jaffa cakes to the passengers. They were quickly taken from him and he was urged to turn round and "FLY THE BLOODY PLANE", this he did, but we went back into rollercoaster mode. It was the worst hour of my life and has made me shit scared to fly ever since, which is a bit strange for someone who has flow all over the world and actually jumped out of a perfectly good airplane during my parachute course. If the fear had of been uncontrollable then the stench would have been unbearable, as the aircraft didn't even have a toilet. Thank God it was only a short flight, even though it did feel like a lifetime. We eventually landed at Sydney Airport, relieved, and helped the pilot unpack our bags. We spent 5 days at the conference and the Canadians were great hosts constantly providing us with huge Lobsters and Steak.

I planned to make the most of my trip to Canada by taking some leave in Halifax at the end of the trip, this time we hired a car and drove for eight hours to reach our destination! My wife and I had a wonderful stay in Halifax and prepared to fly home; we were upgraded to first class and bought live Lobsters to take back with us. The flight to the UK was a direct flight between Halifax and Glasgow and we actually did board an Air Canada 737, I was nervous walking past all the smaller aircraft to get to it thought. The flight seemed to be going fine and we were being pampered by the First Class cabin crew when it was announced that we had to alter course and land in Reykjavik in Iceland. We were then asked to depart the plane for the terminal I was staring to panic Air Canada had done this to me before; they had taken me off a big plane and made me get on a little one in Halifax. It was only when we reached the First Class lounge that we realised why we had deviated from our route. It was the morning of September 11th 2001 and because of the terrible attacks on the twin towers in New York the Americans had shut down their airspace and ordered everything to land, even the aircraft that were flying away from American. After a couple of hours we were allowed to re-embark our 737 and continue to Glasgow, everyone was discussing the terrible events in New York and just wanted home. We arrived in Glasgow, were picked up and drove the 20 or so miles home only to get there and find that my wife had left her handbag at the airport with our keys in it. When we got back to Glasgow airport part of it was cordoned off due to a terrorist alert. It appeared to the vigilant security staff at the airport that some devious enemy, who were now apparently Al Qaeda, may be trying to blow up the airport with a bomb in a handbag. It took us some time and a lot of explaining but we were able to get the bag back after a lecture from the Police and airport security. Of all the days my wife could have chosen to leave a bag unattended it was on that infamous day, she's never done that again though. We arrived home and watched the shocking scenes being played over and over on the TV.

For me it was back to work in the operations room. One month after my return he opportunity presented itself to move to HM Coastguard training Centre as a Learning and Development Consultant (Instructor), I took the chance and we were all set to move to Highcliffe in Dorset.

CHAPTER 21

Ꮒighcliffe and beyond part 2

Despite the promises to my wife that the move to Dorset would be beneficial to both my career and us as a family, I don't think she believed me when she arrived at our new house. You could view our new property in two ways, either the back bedroom had no floor or, my chosen perspective the kitchen had a very high ceiling! There was no carpet, no central heating and for two weeks only microwaves to cook with, my two children were like Pavlov's dogs responding to the 'ding' of the microwave. One week after we arrived I went off to Yarmouth for a week, to deliver training; my wife didn't even know where all the shops were. Part of my role at the training centre was to market, sell and deliver training to external organisations and in particular to foreign nations, for a Civil Servant that is not particularly easy as often business will be done over a restaurant table or at sporting events, both breaks the Civil Service code. One of the nations who agreed that the UK deliver training to their Coastguard was a key Middle East state. My two colleagues and I researched the needs of the students and had to ensure that the meat they would eat at the chosen location, in Falmouth, Cornwall, was certified Halal. After being told that the group was deeply religious we worked with a national Muslim group to ensure that a suitable room was available for prayers and altered the training course to facilitate prayer time. The candidates were very enthusiastic and hard working and every night got taxis to Plymouth to visit bars, clubs and to utilise the other types of entertainment that Plymouth has provided for sailors since its inception! The candidates also seemed to want to buy every electronic device that Dixons had in stock. They would return to the hotel in the very early hours each morning, smelling of alcohol and 'unload' taxis with all sorts of electrical goods. Having spent time with my colleague from Iraq, I was under the impression that devout Muslims did not drink alcohol; these guys must have thought that prohibition was imminent with the amount of Whisky they brought back from Plymouth. At the end of the 3 week course they offered me a gift as a souvenir, Civil Servants aren't allowed to accept gifts, so I had to decline the offer and explain why I had offended them, they accepted my reasoning and gave the Tag Huer watch to the Manager of the hotel. In the end they presented the organisation with a small crystal statue.

I had the opportunity to attend a major international exercise planning meeting in Barbados, the focus was to try and secure training which could be provided by the UK. I left Gatwick and flew to Grantley Adams International Airport in Bridgetown, Barbados. Upon arrival I was met by a British Consulate driver and taken to my hotel. I would be in Barbados for 5 days and wasn't dressed for the daytime weather, I had only my Coastguard uniform which was designed for the UK, for 5 days I resembled the incredible melting man. At one stage a French delegate asked me if I was ok, as he noticed me sweating profusely and thought I was having either a coronary or was about to faint. The walk from the air-conditioned hotel to the air-conditioned car was less than 20 feet but as soon as I exposed myself to the sunlight it was a case of 'whoosh', soaked, as if someone had thrown a bucket of water over me, I was like a bloody vampire trying to stay out of the sunlight. I must have lost 3 or 4 Lbs just through sweating. None of the other delegates seemed to want to sit next to me during meetings and when I unpacked my bag at the end of the trip I knew why.

We quickly made new friends in Christchurch, Dorset and like many families we would visit the local pub before Sunday lunch. On one occasion my wife left to put the Sunday lunch on and I stayed behind, a gentleman entered the pub trying to sell the biggest white fluffy rabbit you have ever seen, with a few beers in me, I bought it for the kids! It was more like a small dog than a rabbit it really was massive, but it appeared to be very aggressive, I put this down to the fact that it had moved home and everyone knows moving house is stressful! On the Monday I went to London for a week, my wife phoned me at teatime going berserk as our huge big fluffy, aggressive rabbit had turned into 14 rabbits, the bugger was pregnant, and that was why it was so big and aggressive. As soon as I got back from London I built a rabbit run that was the size of a small car park. The rabbit, who the kids had christened 'Lady' simply didn't like humans especially small ones who wanted to pick her up all the time, she scratched and bit the kids at every opportunity, they loved it but also hated it at the same time. She had to go, but how and where to. With my inherited guile I hatched a plan, the local school had a pet adoption scheme so I decided to give them 14 rabbits, however it wasn't likely that they would take them all, so one night I chased the rabbits around the run and eventually got them all into a large cardboard box. I carried them to the school opposite with the box bouncing all over the place and emptied them over the fence into the school grounds. The next morning our eldest noticed the vacant rabbit run and asked where they could have possibly gone, we told him they had gone to Scotland to visit his auntie. Two days later in school there were 14 new photographs on the 'pet wall' our eldest informed the teacher that he had 14 rabbits and they looked like those in the photographs, but they couldn't be his, as his rabbits had gone to visit family in Scotland. Every time my wife picked him up from school she was convinced the staff were talking about her and rabbits in the same breath, she never went to a parents night, I had to do them alone!

The Maritime and Coastguard Agency (MCA), who are the parent agency for HM Coastguard had a new Chief Executive who in an instant decided that we were not to market the expertise and skills of UK Coastguards to other countries and therefore disbanded the team. This was strange as we had build up an extremely good international portfolio and reputation. We all returned to the main cadre of training centre as instructors. Putting things in context that Chief Executive did not remain with the organisation very long, and given that his title Captain and his name was Bligh it is hardly bloody surprising. The maritime media and staff had a field day during his tenure and following his departure. The 'Wider Markets' team, as we were known, was never re-established.

Going back to the Training Centre was still a good move, we got to interact with all those passing through the centre and with such a small workforce we got to know a fair percentage of those within the service. There are, at the time of writing, less than 600 full time regular Coastguard Officers. For an Island nation with nearly 11,000 miles of coastline and 13 million visitors to the seaside every year that's pretty incredible. There are more registered, Neurosurgeons, thatchers, white witches and according to a census more Jedi Knights in the UK, than Coastguards. Trainees would often gather on a Sunday evening at a particular pub in Mudeford, near the training centre for the Karaoke. It not that they were particularly adept at singing it was the other participants, one older couple would hog the microphone they had this deluded idea that they were good, they were atrocious. The gentleman had a lisp and Coasties would ask him to sing such classics as 'Spanish Eyes' or 'Sunshine Girl' in fact they requested anything that had an S in the title and spent the rest of the night practising urine retention, is was a scream. They got a laugh and the elder couple got beer, it was fair trade in my eyes.

The Training Centre had a single perimeter fence and a remotely operated barrier as security and was subject to the same alert state as all Government sites. To me it seemed perverse, that this site and GCHQ (the Governments listening Centre) could be given the same security alert state. I had visions of our new enemy Al Qaeda turning up at the barrier and thinking "shit the barrier is down, right lads that was a wasted journey, we'll have to go home", what a deterrent. Imagine the devastation it would have caused to the nation if the site, which was not staffed at night, had been attacked we would have lost all those exam papers! GCHQ it was not.

Staff at the Training Centre undertook key holder duties and the duty member of staff would lock all the buildings, set the alarm and close the main gates. On duty one night I went around every building and made sure the offices were vacant and then locked up, I done this for the whole of the site and eventually locked the main gates and went home. Imagine my surprise when a Coastguard Station phoned me to ask if I was the duty key holder, I replied yes and they then proceeded to explain that an engineer had been in the lavatory and had been locked in one of the buildings. He had heard someone shout something but was more interested in doing the paperwork in the cubicle, than answering, bet he doesn't do that again! He had no number for anyone so done the right thing he rang 999 and asked for the Coastguard. The call was answered with the Coastguard operator asking questions to try and validate the callers claim that he was locked in the Coastguard Training Centre, they then rang the staff of the site to find out who was on duty, after tracing me down they asked that I returned to the site and release my 'prisoner'.

In 2003 the MCA went through another of its regular reviews and re-structuring as a result of a 'management paper' and some roles were lost with new roles and a new concept of operations established. I applied for one of the new posts and was told I had passed the promotion board but the posts I had applied for had all been filled with other candidates, I was pissed off to say the least. However I receive a call from the then Chief Coastguard to say that the post at MRCC Liverpool had not been filled and would I accept that post I said yes, but political correctness and the Civil Service mindset kicked in. Because I had not put MRCC Liverpool down as one of my original choices I was told that I could not have the post and that this post would have to be re-advertised, applications sifted and then interviews to take place, just one of the less cost effective Civil Service way of doing things. I submitted the same application and answered the same questions at the promotion board, was told I was successful and then offered the post, I accepted again and that was it. We were off to Liverpool.

CHAPTER 22

North West and beyond

I arrived at MRCC Liverpool to take up my new post as Area Operations Manager for the North Wales and North West area. This stretched from the Mull of Galloway in Scotland to Ffriog in mid Wales and included liaison with the Isle of Man. It had two MRCCs one at Liverpool and one at Holyhead on the island of Anglesey. There were 52 full time staff and nearly 500 volunteer Coastguard Officers. Northerners have a reputation for being down to earth these guys and girls were no different and I can work in an environment where people are straight with each other and are not scared to speak their mind.

One of the first major incidents I dealt with was in February 2004, the incident would become infamous around the world, see Government create another agency, highlight the lack of communication between Government agencies and Local Authorities and see people prosecuted. There were positives that also came from, what became known as, the 'Morecambe Bay Cockling Tragedy' an event which cost 23 Chinese nationals their lives. All the rescuers involved and supporting agencies done a spectacular job in responding to one of the most horrific scenes they had ever witnessed. Despite being cold, wet, hungry and tired they worked tirelessly to ensure that they could rescue as many people as possible and to try and recover all those who perished. This event would see many of those involved receive commendations for their actions and efforts. Some would also suffer from mild Post Traumatic Stress Disorder; others would leave their respective services. At the end of a 24 hour incident and lengthy police investigation and trial the Gangmasters Licensing Authority was established, a greater amount of co-operation between Government agencies and Local Authorities in the form of intelligence gathering and sharing and a number of persons went to prison. The regular and volunteer officers of HM Coastguard who participated in this desperate incident were recognised with a Chief Coastguard Commendation for Meritorious Service. One of the most difficult aspects of the evening in question was the fact that some of those who made their way ashore did not want to be found, they were illegal immigrants. Having gone through a traumatic experience they did not relish the thought of giving themselves up to the abundance of 'yellow jackets' on the foreshore. They didn't know whether they were Immigration Officers, Police Officers or Rescuers it must have been a terrifying experience.

The next major catastrophe which the Coastguard in the area dealt with was in January 2005 when the heavens opened up and basically sank areas of Cumbria, they were the worst floods the county had experienced for a generation. On the evening that the major emergency was called declared we I along with another colleague left Liverpool to go to Carlisle, despite the pouring rain and the fact that we had our 'Blue lights' on idiots were overtaking us on the M6 motorway, some drivers clearly knew that every policeman in the NW was assisting the populous of Cumbria. We arrived in Carlisle to a sight that most of us had never witnessed before and frankly didn't want to witness again. A Police Officer indicated that the rendezvous point was Carlisle Castle on the other side of the City from the M6 so we set off through the water, which was over the bonnet of the vehicle, it was obvious we were not going to be able to take the 'normal' route to the castle and decided the route through a shopping centre. We entered the darkened precinct and slowly attempted to make our way to the exits on the other side only to have a conscientious security guard wade thigh deep through the water to tell us that we couldn't drive through the precinct as it was only pedestrians that were allowed in the centre. We commended him on staying at his post and trying to fulfil his duties in such difficult circumstances, but also pointed out that he was being a prat, we were not going to knock anyone over, this was late at night and there was water everywhere. He dwelled on this advice for a minute and then told us as every shop was closed it should be ok! He then guided us to an exit which had steps and a small walkway to cater for those with mobility difficulties; again we had to explain that this was a Toyota Colorado and could neither get down the steps into the flooded street nor down the walkway. Events had taken their toll, he wasn't thinking straight, he eventually gathered himself and took us to an appropriate exit and we made our way to the Castle, leaving behind a very cold wet, tired and bemused Security Guard.

One evening when our crews were out rescuing people and passing provisions to those who had chosen to stay in their homes when a crew noticed an ambulance man and police officer wading down the middle of a street. The crews told them to stay near to buildings as it was safer, the ambulance man informed them that he was local to the area and knew it well so he was ok, as he finished his sentence he disappeared from view quickly followed by the Police Officer. They quickly surfaced and helped by the Coastguard crew and made their way to the side of the street. They had both walked over a hole that under normal circumstances would have had a manhole cover on it. He might have known the area but wasn't too familiar with the location of large drains, Coastguard knew they weren't normally by buildings and if they were you could at least grab onto something.

The residents of Carlisle showed that true British "Dunkirk Spirit" and helped each other; however when the call went out for all those with boats. Etc. to report to a certain location things nearly went array. Some of the objects which resident brought to the scene were questionable some of them were certainly not boats and some of those that could liberally fit that bill were hardly inflated and wouldn't have been safe to use, imagine the efforts we had to put in to convinced well meaning citizens that they were going to cause more grief than good. One individual from another emergency service was very peeved and was heard to comment:

"Bloody Coastguards what do they know about rescuing people in town centres" the answer in short was not very much. But as God had decided that Carlisle would, for a time, become the Atlantis of the North were better placed than he and his colleagues to help, there certainly weren't any fires!

Once the flood water had receded it was time for the Coastguards to leave and around three weeks after the event I received a phone call from a gentleman complaining that Coastguards had damaged him car, he wasn't happy and wanted his car repaired. After a prolonged conversation with the irate individual it became apparent that his vehicle had received a scuff mark and may have been caused by Coastguards. The mark was on the roof of his vehicle the only problem was if the damage had indeed been caused by Coastguards it could only have been caused by one of our boats, as his car was underwater at the time of the incident. Colleagues in the other emergency services had also received similar calls; it remains to be proved whether or not there originated from the same person. Needless to say the gentleman was advised to claim off his own insurance.

In 2007 over 100 Coastguards assisted the authorities in Gloucestershire during the flood which devastated that county. A number of Coastguard

Response Vehicles (CRV) were sent to facilitate humanitarian assistance, this took the form of delivering bottled water to vulnerable residents. I am sure the residents of Gloucestershire were aware the situation was dire, but I think one or two must have considered things worse than first thought when vehicles with 'HM Coastguard' emblazoned on them, drove though villages and towns, you don't normally see them in land. The Local Authority had an extensive list of vulnerable persons, however given the conditions that prevailed in the county there were more than were listed. For example Mrs Miggins may have been a spritely, healthy 85 year old under normal circumstances, however when you place 6 foot of water in her living room she becomes vulnerable believe me. We identified special sites and individual residents could also ring for water to be delivered. One elderly lady contacted us, she was obviously and 'imperial' baby as she asked if she could have 450 litres of bottled water delivered, when asked why she required such an amount she said that she wanted to bake a cake for her helpers. She had either got her litres and millilitres mixed up or was trying to get into the Guinness Book of Records for baking the world's biggest sponge cake under extreme conditions.

One nursing home called and requested water for the residents and the closing comment from the lady making the order was:

"Can you send that sexy little Welsh lad with it?" we had a number of volunteers from Wales; none were particularly sexy or little! We had to tell the Lady we would try but explained that we were very busy and couldn't guarantee her request, she told us not to worry just to leave it until he was available. We had to draw lots, but delivered the water and there were no complaints so we either got the right individual or someone got a big ego boost. After 10 days of hard graft and sleeping on the floor of a garage all the Coastguards returned home, safe in the knowledge that they had once more proved to how adaptable, innovative and committed they were. At one stage they were delivering between 35-45 tonnes of water to the people of Gloucestershire all in 1 litre bottles that were loaded and unloaded by hand. Once more their efforts were recognised in the form of a Chief Coastguard Commendation for Meritorious Service.

HM Coastguard is the only emergency Service that are authorised to 'March past' the Cenotaph, alongside the armed forces and veterans on Remembrance Sunday. This is due to the fact that during the First World War three ships HMS Aboukir, HMS Cressy and HMS Hogue, crewed entirely by Coastguards, who had been mobilised into the Royal Navy, were sunk with nearly 1400 Coastguards perishing. It is rumoured that, what is now (at the time of writing), the MCA Training Centre was used as a temporary morgue for those poor souls. For many modern day Coastguard Officers attending the cenotaph is a huge honour, for me as a senior officer it was an even greater honour to 'Command' the Coastguard party. HM Coastguard is a totally civilian force and nowhere in the terms & conditions of staff does it state they have to be able to march. For the former Royal Marine who was teaching them drill prior to the Cenotaph this is a challenge, to say the least. He had one week to prepare 12 individuals to 'move as a disciplined body', as a former military instructor it is hard to 'teach' drill without raising your voice, you have to bark orders, it wouldn't be the same politely asking a group of civil servants to 'right wheel please'. But he endured and eventually was able to bring some order to what was the chaos of the first day. In fact there had to be an official circular put out to remind staff that if they wanted to attend in the future they must have sensible footwear and not high heels, I assume that this directed at female staff, but the civil service is a diverse organisation so I can't confirm that. Suffice to say thank God the cold war was over because if we had been seconded to the Royal Navy we would have lost the war if there was a 'march off'.

In 2005 the same drill instructors task became even bigger. HM Coastguard also have a set of 'Colours' like many military organisations, this is again due to their involvement and sacrifice in the First World War and over 180 Coastguard were to participate in a major event at which the 'Colours' of HM the Queen would be presented by our Honorary Commodore and the Queens representative HRH Prince Charles. Coastguard came from all over the country and were paraded in what was effectively 3 divisions representing Scotland and Northern Ireland Region, East of England Region and Wales and Western England Region, I was once more honoured to be chosen to lead the Wales and Western England region contingent. After a week of practise the event took place and went to plan, however after the parade my wife and I were talking to a very Senior Coastguard Officer who had commented on how well we had all done. However his experience on the day had been ruined by some 'brat' behind him talking and emptying a bag of crisps over his head and uniform, he was livid. I never had the heart to tell him that the brat in question was my two year old daughter, who had no interest in the celebrations. After the parade his Royal Highness and his wife circulated amongst the gathered Coastguards and as he approached my wife and I, I was informed in no uncertain terms what would happen to me if I made her laugh, I didn't. She had eventually got to meet the Royals. The Royal Party make pleasant conversation with us and then departed, he never once mentioned that my backside used to belonged to his Mum.

CHAPTER 23

Funny things happen at sea

Whilst the nature of the job of a Coastguard means there will inevitably be incidents with fatalities there are also incident which remain vivid memories for Coastguards due to their uniqueness or humour, each and every Coastguard will have such a tale to tell, this chapter mentions but a few of those which from personal experience were funny, at least they were at the time.

Imagine it is a blustery afternoon on the West Coast of Scotland during the school holidays. Suddenly a call is received from Glasgow Airport to say that an aircraft approaching the airfield had reported sighting a life raft in the Firth of Clyde, the position was given. The Operations Room team spring into action gathering more information, broadcasting to shipping asking them for more information and to keep a sharp lookout for the life-raft and any survivors. The mood in the operations room is tense, one of the operators is hunched over a chart of the area and in the process of defining a search area considering the target type and prevailing weather conditions. At the same time one of his colleagues is starting to task Lifeboats and Helicopters to the scene. This has all happened within 10 minutes of the first phone call. A ship calls in to report that he can see some fish crates on the surface in the area that the life raft was first reported, the tension increases. The VHF radio cackles into life and a helicopter reports it can see the life raft in the distance, all units are diverted to this position, the anticipation of a successful rescue increases. The helicopter then reports that the wind is causing the life raft to continuously 'tumble' across the surface. The tension increases again, have survivors been thrown out of the life raft? The helicopter arrives on scene and reports that the life raft is actually a Bouncy Castle. The tension subsides and a chuckle reverberates around the room. Details are gathered and the owner of the bouncy castle is contacted, does he thank us for returning his children's plaything? No, he tells us that if the story gets into the newspapers he'll sue us, our press office don't care and put out a press release.

One of the systems used by mariners to broadcast distress alerts if called Digital Selective Calling (DSC) and there are Short Range (VHF), Medium Range (MF) and Long Range (HF) systems in place. One evening the DSC terminal started to indicate an alert had been broadcast on MF DSC, we took the details and plotted the position of the ship, which was in the Black Sea some miles off Sevastopol. We then awaited the response of the Russian Coastguard station in Odessa, no reply came. We acknowledged the distress, quickly identified the telephone number for the Russian station and proceeded to ring them. The phone was answered by what appeared to be a very irate female Russian Coastguard at the end of the phone, the problem was she couldn't speak English or Welsh for that matter and I couldn't speak Russian so we could not communicate, which wasn't good, nobody else had replied to the distressed ship which had indicated it was sinking. I recalled hearing of a Volunteer Coastguard on the Shetland Isles who could speak a silly number of languages, could he speak Russian? I decided to contact Shetland Coastguard and they knew exactly who it was and asked him to phone me back. He contacted us we gave him the questions to ask and the Russian phone number. After what seemed a lifetime he called us back to say the information had been passed to the Russian Coastguards and they were affecting a rescue. He also informed us the number we had given him was a shop and the lady owner was very annoyed that some English person (the lady had obviously never spoke to someone from Belfast before) had woke her up at silly o'clock. But she provided the number for the Russian Coastguard Station and they got onto it, rescuing all those on board the Russian ship, which was a total loss. The newspaper headlines the next day read 'Vladi Lucky', and they were. Remember in the past I had trained to shoot communist hordes that were standing still at 100 yards and 'march' them off the parade square, how life had changed.

Whilst in Australia with the Royal Navy There was an Australian Navy Frigate berthed in front of us the crew were going about their usual business of maintaining the ship and training. One of the deck crew was in a Bosuns chair which was dangling at the stem of the ship and he was merrily painting the stem. His colleagues on deck were obviously painting the upper deck, I watched in slow time as they progressed towards the forward end of the deck painting bollards and fittings. As the deck team approached the foredeck they undid a line on a set of bollards in slow motion there was a muffled scream and the guy painting the stem plummeted into the harbour, they had forgot their colleague was attached to the line. The Australian sailors rushed around throwing lifebelts and trying to recover their mate, the British submariners went into fits of laughter!

During my time with the RAF in Tenby we had a new deckhand join the unit. Like every new recruit he was keen and conscientious every task and order was carried out to the letter. One evening we were acting as a range clearance vessel to ensure a firing range was safe to use, we were working with another vessel. The evening passed without incident and the order came through to head for home, so we duly set a course for Tenby at one stage the new deckhand was told to follow a set of red lights as they indicated the safe route. The rest of the crew were stowing equipment and making a brew when the boat suddenly ground to a halt throwing everyone forward, it was like a bad B movie with the whole crew lurching forward two or three foot. Once the shock of the event had been overcome we all rushed to the wheelhouse to find out what the hell happened. It turned out that the deckhand in question had got the wrong set of red lights the ones he was following belonged to a Landover which was recovering a RHIB, when it left to join the road the new deckhand had inadvertently tried to follow it and had run the boat aground up a beach! We were lucky it was low tide so we just had to wait for 6 hours to float the boat off, the new deckhand re-mustered shortly afterwards to become a photographic interpreter with the RAF. The RAF never knew.

Coastguards will deal with many incidents every year were vessels have either broken down or run out of fuel. During one such incident a colleague asked all the relevant details of the vessel and crew such as how many people onboard, where they had left, where they were bound and established the position of the stricken vessel. A lifeboat was then sent to give the vessel and her stricken crew a tow back to port. Now you have to remember that RNLI crews are also volunteers, they leave their place or work or the comfort of their home to crew Lifeboats. On this particular occasion the boat attached a tow to the yacht and reported that they would tow the broken down vessel to the lifeboats home port. Within minutes the owner of the yacht was on the radio complaining that the lifeboat was not towing him to his desired destination. We explained that this was normal procedure, at which stage a very snooty leisure mariner informed all and sundry on the radio that he had made donations to the RNLI for over 30 years and that this was unacceptable. Apparently and RNLI crew member told him to remember that they were not the AA and that he should go away in short jerky movements, better still he should get his yacht serviced on a regular basis.

A fellow submariner would, when overseas, be consistently unfaithful to his wife, not unique and I am certainly not going to question his morals as he had an agreement and open relationship with his wife. As long as he did not look at the face of his female companions it was agreed that he could be unfaithful. His chosen position was therefore from behind or 'doggy fashion' as it is commonly known. After a particularly long deployment his submarine was scheduled to stay in port for three weeks, he quickly got himself into a 'short term' relationship with a local lady. After about two weeks he was making love to the lady in question when she pleaded with him to let her look at her when they were in the throes of passion he assured her it would happen next time. The next time they got together he demanded his favourite position and she demanded to see his face, so he compromised. He got out his ID card and placed it in front of her face and carried on from behind, now that's a compromise!

All servicemen and women will tell you the worst kick to moral is not the lack of real food, it's not the uncomfortable conditions, it's not even the enemy attacking you . . . . it's the 'Dear John' letter. I am thankful my parents didn't name me John to have every letter start that way would have been a nightmare. There are two names you do not want to name your children if you want them to join the armed forces one is John (because they will always get jilted) the other is Will. If you have ever seen a war film or have ever been in the armed forces 'Fire at Will' is an actual order, poor bastard, I don't know what he's done. but somewhere in history he's pissed someone off. Servicemen and women can deal with adversity, they're trained to do that, one of the best retorts I have ever heard to a 'Dear John' went like this. A young sailor had dedicated his time and most of his salary to provide for his girlfriend at home, unfortunately she had used the money he had sent home to pamper herself and 'party', as a result she had met a new 'beau' and finally realised that her new relationship was what she wanted. She penned a 'Dear John' explaining how he was wonderful, too good for his own good, she was bad and that she really didn't deserve him and as such their relationship was over. He was distraught; however, like all good buddies his mates rallied round and supported him. He asked all his shipmates' if they had photographs of wives and girlfriends and of course most did. He gathered up nearly 30 photographs of wives and girlfriends in various states of undress, from his mates, and sent them in a letter to his 'ex', he stated in the letter that he was sorry to hear their relationship had ended but was unsure which of his girlfriends she was, therefore could she please remove her photograph from the collection he had sent and return the remaining photographs in the stamped addressed envelope that he had provided . . . . touché tart!

After one particularly nasty incident in which a number of Russian seamen perished I was 'defusing' at home, with a glass of wine, when I received a telephone call, around 10:45 at night and was gobsmacked that the caller was actually the Russian Ambassador to the UK. He was ringing to personally and asked me to pass his heartfelt thanks to all those involved in the incident for their effort, this was a completely unsolicited call and took me by surprise. I am a simple Coastguard, I do not normally mix in such circles so was surprised that 1) That he had my phone number and 2) He had phoned me direct. In the cold light of day the answers soon became apparent he had found my contact details on the internet and whilst very sincere I believe he was phoning direct because one of the RAF helicopter aircrew was none other than Flight Lieutenant Wales, or HRH Prince William as he is known to those who are not in the RAF. But progress is progress, to think that 28 years ago I was training to fight off the Communist hordes, or at least slow them down a little bit, and here was the Russian Ambassador ringing me at home, he also wrote a letter of thanks! The cold war was definitely over.

CHAPTER 24

Nick names and silly games

The forces are known for giving people nick names and one mistake can brand you for the rest of your service career. Most nick names are linked to famous people, some are a play on words and some are just down to something daft that you have done. There are also the generic nicknames that you would expect like Paddy, Jock and Taff, why those from England never got one I don't know maybe it's because there were more of them than us. Nicknames like tattoos are a way of becoming an individual in a very structured environment, they humanise you. One of the most memorable nicknames I heard, and it was given within 24 of a recruit joining, was 'Kneecap', unfortunately the poor guys surname was Cartlidge. I also worked with a guy whose surname was Tickle (he pronounced it Tic hell), he was christened Tess by his colleagues, he hated it but he still answered to it and it soon became the norm. I'll endeavour to give some explanations as to how these names come about, the list is not exhaustive would be simply too big to catalogue, therefore I just try to give one example of common ones. Here goes!

Arthur —For surname Daly—named after the character played by George Cole in the 80's TV series Minder.

Bunny —For surname Warren—named after the place where rabbits live.

Chalky —For surname White—self explanatory.

Denzel —For surname Washington—after the Hollywood movie star.

Errol —For those with the surname Flynn—after the Hollywood movie star.

Frank —For those with the surname Spencer after the 1970s TV comedy character played by Michael Crawford.

Geordie —For anyone from the North East of England (this could seriously piss those off who were from South Shields!)

Happy —For those with the surname Day or Days after the 1980s TV programme featuring Henry Winkler as the Fonz.

Indiana —For those with the surname Jones after the Raiders of the Lost Ark character, made famous by Harrison Ford.

Joe —For those with the surname Mercer, after the famous jockey.

Kinky —For those with the surname Kincaid, or just sexually dirty buggers!

Lemon —For those with the first name Keith, after the comedy persona created by Leigh Francis.

Magnet —For those good looking or smooth talking buggers that always seem to get women (short for Fanny Magnet)

Noddy —For those with the surname Holder, after the lead singer in the 1970s glam rock group Slade.

Oliver —For the hungry bugger, who always asked for more food

Percy —For those with the surname Thrower, after the famous TV gardener.

Quincy —For Medical staff, after the American TV series Quincy MD.

Rambo —For any bugger that could hold his own in a punch-up or those that couldn't but were constantly fighting.

Spud —For those with the surname Murphy—after the Irish nickname for potatoes.

Tommo —For those with the surname Thompson

Victor —For grumpy buggers—after the TV character Victor Meldrew.

Whiskey —For those with the surname Walker—after the famous whisky brand.

Whilst most of the aforementioned are related to surnames and many of those tagged with such nomenclatures probably haven't even heard of those who have caused the denial of their birth names! There are so many nicknames used in the forces, a book could probably be written on them alone. I remember one RAF lad getting christened 'Bambi' because of the way he danced at NAAFI discos and another becoming Oddball, as he reminded everyone of the unique character played by Donald Sutherland from the film Kelly's Heroes. Believe me one mistake or cock up and you're named for life.

The Armed Forces are renown for enjoying a good time and the social aspect of the services is excellent, especially if you are away from your base and on someone else's 'turf'. RAF Mountbatten had the usual NAAFI bar but also a sailing club, which opened at weekends and was the place to be. It is not that this bar was more austere than the NAAFI or bigger, its attraction was simple, the beer was cheaper and any profits went back to the members not some national company. The licensing laws appeared to be more flexible also! One of the guys who owned his own boat would also 'ferry' people back and forth from the Barbican in Plymouth. The Barbican had numerous pubs and we would arrange 'Barbican runs', this entailed trying to have a drink in every pub in the area and at the time there was about 20, very few completed this and I wasn't one of them. Another 'haunt' of the RAF sailors and other at Mountbatten was the New Inn pub in Turnchapel, it was within walking distance of the main gate, and the only challenge was that the return journey was uphill. The Barbican would also feature in another career.

Like every crowd of drunks lewd songs were the order of the day and I recall the crew of Sea Otter giving a rendition of the military/rugby club version of Old' MacDonald's Farm to a crowd of stunned patrons eating their Sunday lunch at a pub in Lowestoft, you'd have thought that aliens had landed. We thought we'd get banned, they invited us back, Lowestoft is like that.

Every serviceman and women of the day eventually got to know the game 'spoons'. Believe me you only played this once, unless you were of course on the 'set up' team. Firstly an unsuspecting victim was selected he would then be blindfolded, he was of the opinion that his challenger had also been blindfolded, wrong, his opponent was in on the painful joke. The victim would place a spoon in his mouth and attempt to smack his challenger on the head, the challenger would invariably shout 'ouch' to make out it was painful, of course it wasn't. Because the spoon had been gripped between the lips or teeth it simply pivoted upwards upon touching the challengers head, clearly beer can cloud any recollection you may have had of physics! The challenger would then do nothing, but another member of the 'team' would tap the victim on the head. At first this would be gently but would get progressively harder as the game went on until the victim gave in, he simply couldn't win. I remember the RAF Mountbatten football team playing such a game at RAF Hullavington, at the time home of the RAF Regiment Parachute Squadrons the victim was a Rockape (a member of RAF Regiment) and his own colleagues where in the end, hitting him on the head with a ladle, he just wouldn't give in. Now let's put this in perspective you are new to a Parachute squadron, so you don't want to let your team down so he just kept going. In the end we just had to give up as there was the possibility he would get knocked out and we simply could not keep our laughter in. On service camps news travels fast and this poor guy had drawn quite a crowd, for a short time he became a legend.

Another 'set up' would be enacted upon new recruits joining units from basic training was the Lancaster Bomber. This entailed two people sitting side by side and pretending to be the Pilot and co pilot of a Lancaster, various other participants would strategically place themselves as if the where the gunners etc. This 'crew' would communicate with what can only be described as the 'Tally ho' accent for a time then encourage additional participants including the 'victim' to play the part of the four Lancaster engines. These individuals would rotate their arms as if they were propellers and suddenly the 'pilot would shout 'Fire in engine four' and the whole audience immediately would empty their drinks and occasionally the odd fire extinguisher on the 'victim', gotcha!

CHAPTER 25

Changing times

Like all organisations HM Coastguard and her parent agency, the Maritime and Coastguard Agency (MCA) and department, Department for Transport (DfT) have undergone constant change some small, some which are huge. The MCA, was, when first formed in April 1998, desperately trying to amalgamate the two main operational disciplines of Surveyors and Coastguard, it simply didn't work. So the powers that, be within the organisation, altered their stance and tried to 'integrate' the two main disciplines. Again this didn't work and eventually they had to accept that the two main disciplines could work alongside each other whilst being different.

They really should have taken a leaf out of the military handbook. No service personnel that I know tell anyone they work for the Ministry of Defence (MOD) even thought that is their parent Government Department. There are of course some people who work directly for the MOD and it is right that they state they work in that department as is correct for those who work directly for the DfT. Similarly if you get a group of service personnel together from different branches of the armed forces they will identify themselves as Royal Navy, Army or Royal Air Force. Bring together a group of sailors or soldiers and they will drill down even deeper and identify themselves as submariners, small ships, Fleet Air Arm, Airborne, Royal Artillery, Guards etc. But they all work together when the shit hits the fan, the MCA could have learnt from that instead of trying to force the issue. 'Street cred' is a term that originated in the US but has been encompassed into every aspect of our lives in the UK and HM Coastguard is no different. For many you must have 'walked the walk' before you can 'talk the talk', in other words understand the mindset and experiences of those you work with or more importantly take charge of, in recent years MCA didn't do that well at all. Our the selection of our next permanent CEO after Captain Bligh not only stunned staff but the UK shipping industry, he was a pleasant gentleman but his previous experience for the job was that he was the former CEO of a major Cancer charity. It was during his tenure that saw Coastguard Officers taking strike action and withdrawing their labour for the first time in 184 years, in pursuance of fair pay. It would also see the start of over 3 years of corrosive 'action short of a strike' by many union members, which not only sapped skills but moral. To put this in some sort of context the Government, DfT and the MCA at one stage had to increase the salary of the lowest paid Coastguard Officer to keep them above the National Minimum Wage. Given the training and responsibilities that staff have this was and, to many, still is morally repugnant, but they get on with it. This same individual set in motion a chain of events that would propose a whole different structure and way of working that would, in the view of some professional Coastguard Officers, decimate HM Coastguard. HM Coastguard has always suffered from a very restricted recruiting pool, which were traditionally those leaving the armed forces, particularly the Royal Navy and ex Merchant Navy personnel. Those traditional recruitment pools have diminished with the reduction in the armed forces and the British merchant fleet. In recent years the organisation has seen more and more individuals brought into the upper echelons of the organisation who have no Coastguard background and simply didn't have the 'street cred', which made many staff distrustful of them and must have made it uncomfortable for those brought in, if indeed they cared at all. I recall a National Audit Office representative telling me during a questioning session that he thought we responded to too many false alarms! He didn't understand the unique role fulfilled by the men and women of HM Coastguard. He simply couldn't accept that we have to get someone or something to the scene to confirm that fact.

There are a number of very highly respected senior officers within HM Coastguard who I believe will never progress further within the organisation because they are seen in some quarters as having too much 'street cred', perverse but true. There are a number of true leaders, of both genders, within HM Coastguard that people would follow and be inspired by. They 'talk the talk' and do not use 'management speak'. To these individuals 'Blue sky thinking' is still referred to a good ideas and 'diverse internal stakeholders' are still staff! They have a belief that managers at any level do not have the monopoly on good ideas.

In March 2010 I was diagnosed with cancer and that is the origins of this collection of stories and thoughts. I realised that I needed to document something that my children could read if I departed! Those thoughts and memories were scribbled on to a notepad whilst I was prone during my recovery and the number of stories grew and grew. I then thought 'to hell with this I'm getting better', so I struck a positive mindset and got myself back to work after 10 weeks treatment and a major operation. The 10 weeks off gave me some time to think and I realised for the past 17 years or so I had inadvertently placed my family second to HM Coastguard. The opportunity arose for me to make my mind up on my future when the Coalition Government announced on 22nd December 2011, that it was to embark on a plan to close nearly half of the UKs Coastguard Rescue Centres. The announcement had followed a protracted consultation period which saw numerous campaigns by local Coastguard Stations and communities to save individual stations and the launch of a national campaign. Many of those campaigns were successful but the announcement had caused moral to plummet at those stations earmarked for closure. In my, not unique but, humble opinion the organisation had started to implode. The reasons given was that the new structure and way of working would make HM Coastguard more resilient, provide a greater career structure for staff, address the issue of low pay and allow the organisation to become the best Maritime Safety organisation in the world. In reality it was about helping the Government to reduce the national deficit, to put things in context, in 2007 it was calculated that the cost of keeping HM Coastguard as is, was a one off payment per year by each taxpayer of £1.41! The savings this plan would realise was approximately 4.5 millions of pounds every year for 3 years, a total of 13.5 million pounds.

In a survey of the general public, conducted in 2008, only 51% knew we had a Coastguard service and even fewer knew you could get hold of them by dialling 999, I suppose the various campaigns that tried to glean the support of the public had a limited audience. With hindsight it was obvious that, in general, only the coastal communities would join the fight to save Coastguard stations. In a way the battle was lost before it began, but staffs were valiant to the end. I made the very difficult decision to leave the organisation that had been a mistress to me for the past 17 years.

I have had the pleasure and honour of working with very many regular Coastguard Officers and Volunteers, having trained coastguards from other nations I can state with some authority that HM Coastguard is the best Search and Rescue co-ordination organisation in the world. As an island nation with approximately 13 millions of visitors to our coasts every year it seemed madness to cut the number of Rescue Co-ordination Centres. But that judgement was not made by me it was made by those well above my pay grade. There would have to be a reduction in staff numbers and my mind had been made up to dedicate some long overdue time to my family. There was also the fact that staff were indicating they wanted to leave the service and that two very senior Coastguard Officers were being referred to by their staff on the ground as the Half-wit and the Has-been. It really was time to go.

Throughout my life in uniform I have met a Queen, Prime Ministers, Princes and paupers, some very intelligent people and others who can't understand why their sister has three brothers and they only have two! They had all had an impact in one way of another on my life.

I wish those who will provide rescue co-ordination for our seas and coasts, in the future, all the best. I know they will rise to the challenge as Coastguards always do. Remember 'Coasties can do it in any weather'. Daniel Defoe is quoted as stating "Greater is an army of sheep led by a lion, than an army of lions led by a sheep". Throughout the public consultation on the future of HM Coastguard and following the Ministerial announcement I witnessed the open hearts and souls of Coastguards in both operations rooms and on the coast they are indeed lions. I have served alongside very many Coastguards and respect them all, even those I was not too fond of, for they too had 'walked the walk'. I am honoured to have been able to call you colleagues and privileged to call many of you friend.

Our armed forces and emergency services work miracles every hour of every day, rain, shit or shine. I am blessed to have been part of that fraternity and thank those currently serving, for their efforts on my behalf as a British citizen. Keep up the good work you are second to none, all of you.

I am lucky to a have wonderful family, to have more memories which make me laugh than cry and some that will remain a secret, as they must. I have been blessed to have the experiences I have had, seen the places I have seen and met the people I have met . . . . to all of you thanks.